Helion & Company Limited
Unit 8 Amherst Business Centre
Budbrooke Road
Warwick
CV34 5WE
England
Tel. 01926 499 619
Email: info@helion.co.uk
Website: www.helion.co.uk
Twitter: @helionbooks
Visit our blog http://blog.helion.co.uk/

Text © Stephen Rookes 2023
Photographs © as individually credited
Colour artwork © David Bocquelet, Jean-
    Marie Guillou, Anderson Subtil 2023
Maps drawn by George Anderson © Helion
    & Company 2023

Designed and typeset by Farr out
    Publications, Wokingham, Berkshire
Cover design by Paul Hewitt, Battlefield
    Design (www.battlefield-design.co.uk)

Every reasonable effort has been made to
trace copyright holders and to obtain their
permission for the use of copyright material.
The author and publisher apologise for any
errors or omissions in this work, and would
be grateful if notified of any corrections that
should be incorporated in future reprints or
editions of this book.

ISBN 978-1-804510-14-8

British Library Cataloguing-in-Publication
    Data
A catalogue record for this book is available
    from the British Library

All rights reserved. No part of this
publication may be reproduced, stored in a
retrieval system, or transmitted, in any form,
or by any means, electronic, mechanical,
photocopying, recording or otherwise,
without the express written consent of
Helion & Company Limited.

We always welcome receiving book
proposals from prospective authors.

Front cover artwork: At the end of the
Second World War, the Allied Technical Air
Intelligence Unit (ATAIU) collected a total
of 64 captured and operational Japanese
aircraft, and prepared them for shipment
to Europe for testing. For different reasons
– primarily related to the lack of shipping
space – only four eventually reached their
destination. Instead, most were flight-
tested while still in South East Asia (SEA)
before the ATAIU-SEA was disbanded, at
Seletar Air Base, in Singapore, on 15 May
1946. Subsequently, a number of captured
Japanese aircraft – including at least one
Mitsubishi A6M 'Zero' fighter – was handed
over to the French in Indochina. The fate of
the aircraft collected by the ATAIU-SEA was
thus symbolic of that of numerous Japanese
flying personnel and ground troops that
surrendered in French Indochina: at least
for a while, they served the old colonial
masters, helping them re-establish their
control over this part of the world. (Artwork
by Pablo Patricio Albornoz © Helion &
Company 2023)

CONTENTS

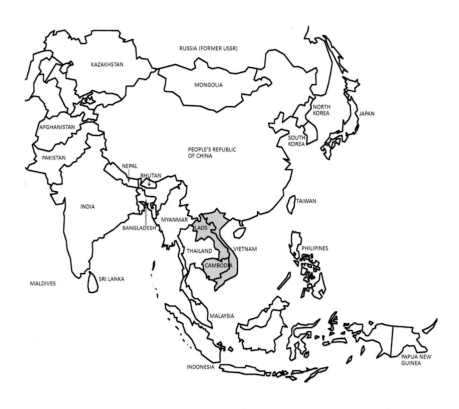

Note: In order to simplify the use of this book, all names, locations and geographic
designations are as provided in *The Times World Atlas*, or other traditionally accepted
major sources of reference, as of the time of described events.

ABBREVIATIONS

AA	Anti-aircraft
AdA	*Armée de l'Air* (French Air Force)
AFV	Armoured Fighting Vehicle
ALAO	*Aviation Légère d'Obsevartion d'Artillerie*
ALFFIC	Allied Land Forces French Indochina
ALFSEA	Allied Land Forces South East Asia
ASEAN	Association of South Eastern Asian Nations
ATAIU	Allied Technical Air Intelligence Unit
AVG	American Volunteer Group
BAIM	*Bataillon Annamite d'Infanterie de Montagne* (Annam Battalion of Mountain Infantry)
BAL	*Brigade d'Annam Laos*
BAPN	*Base Aéroportée Nord*
BAPS	*Base Aéroportée Sud*
BCC	*Brigade de Commandos Coloniaux* (Brigade of Colonial Commandos)
BCCP	*Bataillon Coloniale de Commandos Parachutistes*
BCK	*Bataillon de Chasseurs Khmères*
BCL	*Bataillion de Chasseurs Laotiens*
BCRA	*Bureau Central de Renseignements et d'Action* (Central Bureau of Intelligence and Action)
BDP	*Bataillon de Dragons Portés*
BEAL	*Bataillon Étranger d'Artillerie Légère* (Foreign Legion Artillery Battalion)
BEO	*Brigade d'Extrême-Orient* (Far East Brigade)
BG	*Bataillon du Génie* (Engineering Battalion)
BM	*Bataillon Médical*
BLIM	*Bataillon Laotien d'Infanterie de Montagne* (Battalion of Laotian Mountain Infantry)
BMEO	*Bataillon de Marche d'Extrême-Orient* (infantry)
BMEO	*Brigade Marine d'Extrême-Orient* (Far East Marine Brigade)
BMSEO	*Bataillon de Marche Sénégalais d'Extrême-Orient*
BMT	*Bataillon de Marche du Tchad* (Chad Far East battle group)
BPC	*Bataillon Parachutiste de Choc* (elite paratroop battalion)
CCB	*Compagnie de Commandement du Bataillon* (Battalion command company)
CCP	Chinese Communist Party
CEFEO	*Corps Expéditionnaire Français en Extrême-Orient* (French Far East Expeditionary Corps)
CFLN	*Comité Française de Libération Nationale* (French Committee of Nation Libération)
CLI	*Corps Léger d'Intervention* (Light Intervention Corps)
CMT	*Compagnie Mixte de Transmissions*
CRA/TFIN	*Compagnie de Ravitaillement par Air des Troupes Françaises d'Indochine du Nord*
CRD	*Compagnie Régionale de Défense*
DA	*Division Aéroportée*
DB	*Division Blindée*
DBLE	*Demi-brigade de Légion Etrangère*
DBMP	*Demi-brigade de Marche Parachutiste*
DBSAS	*Demi-brigade Coloniale de Commandos Parachutistes SAS*
DCC	*Division Cochinchine Cambodge*

DIC	*Division d'Infanterie Coloniale*
DICEO	*Division d'Infanterie Colonial d'Extrême-Orient*
DMA	*Détachement Motorisé d'Annam*
DMC	*Détachement Motorisé de Cochinchine*
DML	*Détachement Motorisé de la Légion*
DMT	*Détachement Motorisé du Tonkin*
DRV	Democratic Republic of Vietnam
DT	*Division du Tonkin* (Tonkin Division)
EB	*Escadre de Bombardement*
EC	*Escadrille de Chasse*
EO	*Escadre d'Observation*
ELA	*Escadrille de Liaisons Aériennes*
EMEO	*Escadrille de Marche d'Extrême-Orient*
ER	*Escadrille Régionale*
ERO	*Escadrilles Régionale d'Observation*
EROM	*Escadrille de Reconnaissance d'Outre-Mer*
Esc. C	*Escadrille Coloniale*
ETAP	*Ecole des Troupes Aéroportées*
FAFEO	*Force Aérienne Française d'Extrême-Orient*
FAMIC	*Force Amphibie de la Marine en Indochine*
FAN	*Force Amphibie du Nord*
FAPI	*Formations Aéroportées en Indochine*
FAS	*Force Amphibie du Sud*
FEFEO	*Forces Expéditionnaires Français d'Extrême-Orient*
FFFM	*Flottilles Fluviales de Fusiliers-Marins*
FFI	*Flottille Fluviale d'Indochine*
FIC	French Indochina
FNEO	*Forces Navales d'Extrême-Orient*
GAA	*Groupe Aérien Autonome*
GACI	*Groupe Aérien Centre Indochine*
GANI	*Groupe Aérien Nord Indochine*
GAOA	*Groupe d'Aviation d'Observation d'Artillerie*
GBMS	*Groupement Blindé Mobile Schlesser*
GC	*Groupe de Chasse* (Fighter Group)
GCMA	*Groupement de Commandos Mixtes Aéroportés*
GFTA	*Groupement de Forces Terrestres Antiaériennes*
GLP	*Groupement Léger Parachutiste*
GMEO	*Groupe de Marche d'Extrême-Orient*
GMLE	*Groupe de Marche de Légion Etrangère*
GMTEO	*Groupe de Marche de Transport en Extrême-Orient*
GRC	*Garde Républicaine de Cochinchine*
GT	*Groupe de Transport*
GTF	Gremlin Task Force
GUAL	*Groupement d'Unités d'Armes Lourdes*
HDML	Harbour Defence Motor Launch
IJA	Imperial Japanese Army
IJAF	Imperial Japanese Air Force
IJN	Imperial Japanese Navy
KMT	Kuomintang
LC	Landing Craft
LCA	Landing Craft Assault
LCI	Landing Craft Infantry
LCM	Landing Craft Mechanised
LCVP	Landing Craft Vehicle & Personnel
LCT	Landing Craft Tank
MFV	Motor Fishing Vessel
OSS	Office of Strategic Services

PAVN	People's Army of Vietnam		**RTM**	*Régiment de Tirailleurs Marocains*
RAC	*Régiment d'Artillerie Coloniale*		**RTS**	*Régiment de Tirailleurs Sénégalais*
RACM	*Régiment d'Artillerie Coloniale du Maroc*		**RTT**	*Régiment de Tirailleurs du Tonkin*
RAF	Royal Air Force		**SAL**	*Section d'Avions de Liaison*
RAAF	Royal Australian Air Force		**SAS**	Special Air Service
RC	*Route Coloniale*		**SEAC**	South East Asia Command
RC	*Régiment de Cuirassiers (armoured)*		**SOE**	Special Operations Executive
RCP	*Régiment de Chasseurs Parachutistes*		**SPIN**	*Section de Parachutage d'Indochine du Nord*
REC	*Régiment Etranger de Cavalerie*		**STUP**	*Section Technique des Unités Parachutistes*
REI	*Régiment Étranger d'Infanterie (Foreign Legion)*		**TAIU**	Technical Air Intelligence Unit
RBFM	*Régiment Blindé de Fusiliers-Marins*		**TFIN**	*Troupes Françaises de l'Indochine Nord*
RFM	*Régiment de Fusiliers-Marins*		**TFIS**	*Troupes Françaises de l'Indochine Sud*
RIC	*Régiment d'Infanterie Coloniale*		**US**	United States
RICAP	*Régiment d'Infanterie de Choc*		**USAAF**	United States Army Air Forces
RICM	*Régiment d'Infanterie Chars de Marine*		**USSR**	Union of Soviet Socialist Republics
RMIC	*Régiment Mixte d'Infanterie Coloniale*		**VM**	Viet Minh
RMSM	*Régiment de Marche de Saphis Marocains*		**VP**	*Vedettes de Port*
RTA	*Régiment de Tirailleurs Annamites*		**ZOAL**	Zone Annam-Laos
RTAF	Royal Thai Air Force		**ZOCOC**	Zone Cochinchine
RTC	*Régiment de Tirailleurs Cambodgiens*		**ZOTON**	Zone Tonkin

INTRODUCTION

While the Berlin Conference of 1884–1885 was held to determine which parts of Africa went to which budding, or confirmed, colonial power, towards the end of the 1800s, some of the same colonising nations had been jockeying for position to win trading rights for local resources and raw materials throughout Southeast Asia. Great Britain, for example, had spent the middle part of the nineteenth century attempting to extend its Asian empire eastwards from the Indian subcontinent; the Dutch had been present in what is now Indonesia for the best part of a century; the Philippines had been a Spanish possession since the sixteenth century, and Britain and France fought wars with China so as to obtain increased access to vast supplies of opium and tea, as well as highly cherished commodities such as porcelain and silk.

As for the territories that were eventually united to become Indochina, they had been largely spared from incursions by armies used as proxies to help advance the ambitions of large commercial enterprises such as the British, Dutch and French East India companies. Indeed, though France did seek out commercial opportunities along the Mekong and the Red rivers from the 1850s, French presence in Annam, Tonkin, Cochinchina, Cambodia, and Laos came about largely as a means of protecting the Catholic missionaries of the Paris Foreign Missions Society seen as a political threat to local dynasties, or through the military and political provision of protection of one dynasty from another. Chronologically speaking, the formation of the protectorates took place over a short period of time: Cochinchina was annexed in 1862; Cambodia became a French protectorate in 1863; and by 1886, local opposition to French presence in Tonkin in the north, and Annam in central Vietnam had been overcome. With France also successfully fighting two wars against China as the Berlin Conference was taking place, the various protectorates were unified to become the Indochinese Union in 1887. The French then consolidating their positions, Laos, and the

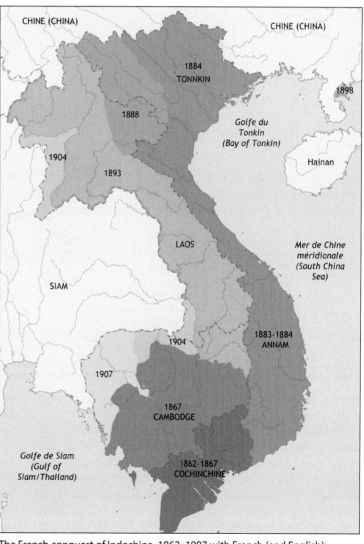

The French conquest of Indochina, 1862–1907 with French (and English) designations of major geographic areas. (Map by Tom Cooper)

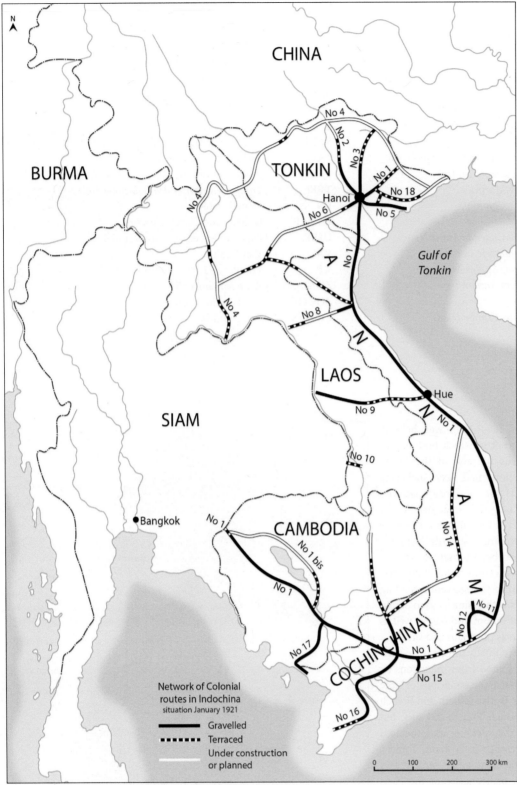

A map of colonial routes in Indochina as of early 1921. (Map by George Anderson)

organisation that possessed a strong political identity, strong political ambitions, plus the political and military tactics necessary for the overthrow of a much larger and more powerful, foe.

The intention of this first volume of three dealing with France's war in Indochina will be to take a closer look at a phase of the war described by Viet Minh leader, Ho Chi Minh, as a fight between the tiger and the elephant. The inference being that war was a tussle that opposed mobility and mass, the phase in question (1946–1949) paved the way for a second period (1950–1954) that saw more regular tactics used on the battlefield; tactics that were deployed at Dien Bien Phu in 1954 and which led to the defeat of French forces.

Of interest to those wishing to increase their knowledge of the First Indochina War or, indeed, the second, as the reader will discover, this first volume does not deal exclusively with 1946 to 1949. Predominantly, this is to provide an explanation for the difficulties France had in overpowering a much smaller enemy as conflict broke out and also to assist the reader in their understanding of the wider geopolitical context in which France's war in Indochina took place. This aspect provides the foundation for further understanding of irregular warfare and the much deadlier conflict fought by the United States and the countries of the Association of South Eastern Asian Nations (ASEAN) in the 1960s and 1970s. Full coverage is given to the main political and military figures who featured during the first phase, as well as the strategies, tactics and weaponry used by both the tiger (Viet Minh) and the elephant (France).

Author's note

While every attempt has been made to provide as comprehensive overview as possible of the First Indochinese War (1946–1949), detailing every operation and listing the movements of every division, regiment, platoon or squad throughout these years, would prove to be a mammoth task taking several months (or years) to complete.

leased Chinese territory of Guangzhouwan then joined the union in the 1890s.

Through France faced many challenges to its authority over Indochina during the coming decades, none would be so great as that posed by an organisation known as the Viet Nam Doc lap Dong minh Hoi, or Viet Minh, in August 1945. In many ways the successors to the organisers of various plots to oppose the French since their arrival, none of the previous attempts to dislodge France from Viet Nam in particular, had amounted to anything more than gestures. The challenge that became apparent in 1945 was, on the other hand, a full-blown armed rebellion carried out by an

Capture of Saigon by France, on 18 February 1859. (Painting by Léon Morel-Fatio; Musée national de la Marine)

A French warship in the port of Tourane, in 1883. (Albert Grandolini Collection)

Obsolete, Chinese-made gun, as captured by the French in the citadel of Son Tay, in 1884. (Albert Grandolini Collection)

1

PRELUDE TO WAR IN INDOCHINA, 1940–1945

The Japanese Invasion of Indochina, September 1940

Although France had possessed one of the world's largest armed forces for over 200 years, the failure of successive French governments to adequately prepare for armed conflict in the 1920s and 1930s, ultimately led to the rapid defeat of their own forces in 1940. The First World War saw 1.4 million French (including colonial troops) die in battle, over 4 million were injured and the effects of the war left scars on the French psyche that would last for decades. Immediately after the war, it was decided that the first global war would be the last and a quest for peace should be prioritised.

This peace was maintained by defending the terms of the Treaty of Versailles of 1919. Defending France from invaders from its eastern and northern borders was, in theory, assured by the construction of the Maginot Line. Built between 1929 and 1938, the line was a series of defences dug deep into the ground that was considered impenetrable. Invading forces would be demoralised by the presence of these defences and the futility of attack, while France's military commanders focused their strategies on the build-up of infantry, artillery and the use of heavy armoury, such as tanks, should any invader still not be deterred. Instead of preparing for more modern forms of war, the aerial forms advocated by military strategists – such as the Italian Giulio Douhet – France stuck to its guns and prepared its aviation for the peaceable pursuits of tourism

and adventure. The failure to build an air force and aviation capable of effectively fighting off the Luftwaffe in May 1940, eventually led to defeat to Nazi Germany in June of that year.

France's defeat led to the resignation of Prime Minister Paul Reynaud on 17 June and on that day, a new cabinet was formed with Marshal Philippe Petain appointed head of a new government, that was to set up in headquarters in the city of Vichy. One of Petain's first tasks was to negotiate an armistice between France, Germany and its allies, including Japan. Seizing the initiative, the same day, Tokyo issued its own demands through the vector of a press conference and through Japan's Vice-Minister for Foreign Affairs, Masayuki Tani. It asked that all weapons cease to be trafficked from Indochina into China. For the Japanese, this was of the utmost importance as since 1939, the United States had been providing assistance to Chinese nationalist leader Chiang Kai-Shek in the form of some 10,000 tonnes per month of military hardware brought into the sea port of Haiphong.[1]

As other conditions were spelt out to the French, such as the closing of the border between China and Indochina and a Japanese commission being sent to supervise the implementation of this specification, the hope being that Japan's objectives were limited to ending its war with China. This did not include expanding its war in the Far East into what was still a French possession.

A Potez 25 of the French Air Force high above Indochina, in 1930. (Albert Grandolini Collection)

Tensions were increasing in French Indochina already before the Second World War. Here a scene from the communist insurrection in the Cochinchina of November 1940. (Albert Grandolini)

Admiral Jean Decoux, who took over from Catroux in July 1940, had 32,000 regulars under his command plus 17,000 auxiliaries capable of putting up a fight, however ill-equipped they may have been.[4] France not quite allied with Nazi Germany at this point and as it was not clear whether Vichy France would join the Allied forces or not, Decoux had also asked for help from the United States and from Great Britain. Nonetheless, both had reservations and limitations on what assistance could be provided and when.

Though further negotiations took place throughout August 1940, any chance of a peaceful outcome was quashed on 6 September 1940, when the 5th Infantry Division of the Imperial Japanese Army's (IJA) Twenty-Second Army crossed the Indochinese border near Dong Dang. Commanded by General Aketo Nakamura and part of the Japanese Southern China Area Army, on 18 September Tokyo informed Decoux that Japan would base 25,000 troops in Indochina, regardless of any prior agreement. Although more negotiations brought this number down to 6,000, the Twenty-Second Army was eager to force the issue through military means. Its troops exchanged fire with French forces based on the border, other border posts were attacked and by 25 September 1940, the French position at Lang Son was forced to surrender. Among the French forces, under General Mennerat, taking part in the fighting was the 2nd Battalion of the 5e *Régiment Etranger d'Infanterie* (5e REI), the 3e *Régiment de Tirailleurs du Tonkin* (3e RTT) and the 9e *Régiment d'Infanterie Coloniale* (9e RIC).

It was a naïve to believe Japan would not seize the opportunity, as not only did Indochina possess significant supplies of rubber, tin, coal and rice found in Indochina, but a further advantage for Japanese military planners was that Indochina could be used as bases from which other Western colonial powers could be attacked.[2] For this reason, on 22 June, the Japanese issued a demand for naval basing rights at Guangzhouwan,[3] followed by demands to set up air bases and the right to transit troops through Indochina. More resistance to the Japanese could, perhaps, have been provided.

While the attacks of French forces were taking place at Dong Dang, an amphibious landing by the Japanese was being prepared. Japanese aircraft from carriers operating around Hainan Island in the Gulf of Tonkin, attacked French positions along the coast south of Haiphong. The aircraft carriers in question were the Hiryu (Flying Dragon) and its sister ship, the Soryu (Blue or Green Dragon).

Troops of the IJA's 5th Infantry Division cross the border into Indochina near Dong Dang in September 1940. (Author's collection)

IJA troops make their way to Lang Son in September 1940 (Author's collection)

IJA troops gather on the Chinese border with Indochina, 21 September 1940 (Author's collection)

The *Hiryu* was built during the mid-1930s for the Japanese Imperial Navy. Her aircraft supported the Japanese invasion of Indochina, and she was later to take part in the attack on Pearl Harbour and the Battle of Wake Island. In February 1942, her aircraft bombed Darwin, Australia.

France did nothing to hinder Japanese interests in the region. An agreement was subsequently reached on 9 December 1940, whereby French sovereignty over administrative operations and its army was confirmed and Japan was authorised to station some 40,000 troops in the country as a base to combat Allied forces.

The reasons for this being that Japan was keeping a close eye on what direction to take in regard to the Soviet threat to the north of its Manchurian territories. Following the Nazi invasion of the Soviet Union in June 1941, Japanese planners decided that it was the right moment to move south and ward off threats of an oil shortage brought on by the possibility of an embargo imposed by the United States. To prepare for an invasion of the Dutch East Indies, an estimated 140,000 members of the IJA invaded Indochina in July 1941. During the invasion, the airfields in Saigon, Tan Son Nhut, Thudamot, and Bien Hoa were occupied along with bases at Soc Trang, Nha Trang and Da Nang (Tourane).

The Franco-Thai War, 1940–1941

In addition to the demands of Japanese ambitions, by October 1940, Vichy France found itself face-to-face with a threat to territories situated in the western areas of Indochina. France being weakened by the defeat to Nazi Germany in June 1940 Europe and subsequent incursions into Tonkin by the IJA from September of that year, Siam (Thailand) chose October 1940 as the time to regain territories ceded to France in the late nineteenth century during the reign of King Chulalongkorn. These territories, mainly situated in Laos and along the banks of the Mekong River, the French had, indeed, been forced to allow Japan to set up military bases the previous month. The Siamese believed that France would not put up any serious military resistance, as at the time, the country's armed forces appeared numerically capable of dominating Vichy France's colonial armies.

Thai Forces in October 1940

At the time the attacks were launched against the French, the Royal Thai Army consisted of around 60,000 men serving in four armies. The largest of these four were the Burapha Army, made up of five

On 26 September, an amphibious landing took place at Dong Tac. Tanks were put ashore, French positions were bombed by the Japanese Army Air Force (JAAF) and by the end of the day, the Japanese had seized control of the Gia Lam Airbase near Hanoi, the rail marshalling yard at Lao Cai and stationed 900 troops in Haiphong, as well as 600 in Hanoi. At this point, Emperor Hirohito ordered fighting to stop as the French had surrendered the previous day.

As the signing of the tripartite act between Japan, Nazi Germany and Italy was taking place on 27 September 1940, Japanese occupation of the southern areas of French Indochina did not take place immediately. Indeed, the Japanese appeared satisfied to leave the framework of Vichy French control in place as long as

Also built during the mid-1930s, the Soryu took part in the Second Sino-Japanese War, the invasion of Indochina plus the attacks on Pearl Harbour, Wake Island and Darwin. As part of Japan's 1st Air Fleet, the Soryu took part in the Battle of Midway in June 1942. It was here that she sank with the loss of over 2,000 crew members.

Until the arrival of the 'Zeke', the A5M4 was the main fighter used by the Japanese Imperial Navy. It entered service in early 1937 and saw action in the Second Sino-Japanese War (1938) against the Republic of China Air Force's Boeing P26-C Model 281. The A5M4's armaments were two 7.7mm (0.303 in) machine guns. (Author's collection)

The Nakajima B5N2 replaced the B5N1, an aircraft that had also seen action in the Second Sino-Japanese War. The B5N2 was equipped with a much more powerful engine (Sakae Model 11, 14-cylinder twin-row radial). A three-man operated aircraft, it carried a Type 92 machine gun in the rear dorsal position and Type 91 torpedoes or bombs. (Author's collection)

Krupp guns. Its armoured force included 20 Vickers 6-Tonners, 35 light Ford vehicles, four Landsverk L-60 tanks, and 60 Carden-Loyd tankettes.

Regarding air power, in December 1940 the newly named Royal Thai Air Force (RTAF) was organised along the lines of Table 1 on the next page.[5]

Vichy French Forces in Indochina, 1940

Note: Translations relating to the names of French units are indicative.

The abbreviations 'e', 'er', and 'ère', are the French equivalents of the English 'st', 'nd', rd, and 'th'.

As for the conflict itself, the number of border incidents along the Mekong River multiplied at the end of October 1940 with the RTAF making a number of incursions into Laos and Cambodia. During November and December 1940, several aerial duels were fought above the disputed territories and on 4 January 1941, Thailand decided to go on the offensive when it became clear that diplomatic negotiations would fail to give back the territories it had previously lost to the French. A Thai squadron attacked Dong Hen airfield in Laos on that day as it was the base for the *Escadrille de Chasse* 2/95 (EC 2/95) and bombing runs over military targets were made on Vientiane, Phnom Penh, Sisophon and Battambang.

French retaliation followed and after French forces attacked the Thai town of Aranyaprathet on 5 January 1941, Thai armies launched an offensive using artillery and bombing of French positions. The offensive covered four fronts: North Laos, where the Thai Army took back disputed territories with little opposition; South

divisions and the Isan Army, with three divisions. In turn, these divisions were divided into 44 battalions of infantry, 13 artillery groups, nine cavalry squadrons (two motorised), six battalions of engineers, one signals battalion, three tank companies and an anti-aircraft company armed with a mixture of 40 and 75mm plus

Laos, where the Thais crossed the Mekong River: the Dângrêk Sector comprising the Dângrêk Mountains (natural border between Thailand and Cambodia); and along *Route Coloniale 1* (RC1) in the Battambang province.

Table 1			
Name	**Composition**	**Base**	**Aircraft**
No 73 Mixed Wing	32nd Observation Squadron and 50th Bomber Squadron	Ubon	9 x V-93S Corsairs, 6 x Martin B-10s (139 W model)
No 35 Mixed Wing	34th Observation Squadron, and 50th Fighter Squadron	Udorn, and Nakhon Phanom	9 x V-93S Corsairs, 9 x Hawk IIIs (Goshawks).
No 66 Wing	Foong Bin Phibun Songkhram Squadrons 1 and 2, 60th Fighter Squadron	Dong Muang (Bangkok)	24 x Ki.30 'Nagoya' (Ann),[6] 11 x Hawk P-36s (model 75N)
No 74 Wing	44th Observation Squadron, 72nd Fighter Squadron, Observation Squadron	Chantaburi	9 x V-93s, 9 x Hawk IIIs
No 74 Mixed Wing	73rd Fighter Squadron (Sisaket), 35th and 80th Fighter Squadrons	Sisaket and Pranchinburi	9 x Hawk IIIs (Sisaket), 9 x Hawk IIIs and 9 V-93Ss at Prachinburi)

Notes: Royal Thai Air Force (RTAF)

Around 70 Avro 504N trainers were delivered in 1930 (20 examples) or built locally (50 examples). The RTAF possessed 12 Curtiss Hawk IIs (all delivered in 1934), 74 Curtiss Hawk IIIs (24 delivered in 1935, 25 built locally in 1937), 25 built locally in 1939). The Hawk IIIs carried the designation Type 10, or Type F-10. There were 12 Curtiss Hawk 75Ns that were all delivered in 1938 and which were designated Type 11, or Type F-11. The six Martins were delivered in 1937 and the RTAF also used Mitsubishi Ki.21s (Sally/Type 97 Heavy Bomber) delivered in December 1940). As for the Vought V-93S Corsairs, 12 were bought in 1933, 25 were built locally in 1936, and 50 more were built locally in 1939. All were designated Attacker Type 1 or A-1. On top of this, the RTAF used 13 Fairchild F-24Js delivered in 1940

Notes: Royal Thai Naval Aviation (RTNA)

The RTNA possessed 6 Watanabe WS.103S Floatplanes delivered in May 1938. Four were based at Sattahip Naval Base southernmost tip of Chonburi Province in Thailand and two on corvettes), 1 Avro 504N delivered by RTAF 1939), and 18 Nakajima E8Ns Type 95 ('Dave') acquired in late 1940.

The Japanese capture Haiphong in July 1941. (Author's collection

River and French naval vessels attacking the Thai Navy in the Gulf of Siam.

The main thrust of the French counter-attack made by forces commanded by Colonel Henri Jacomy, turned out to be a strategic failure. Firstly, the assault force consisting of one battalion of colonial infantry (European) and two battalions of mixed infantry (European and Indochinese) could not be supported by artillery due to the dense forest covering the area; secondly, no air support was provided; and, thirdly, poor radio communications hindered operations. The latter was down to the French using Morse code which enabled the Thai Army to easily intercept operational plans.

Were it not for the 3rd Battalion of the 5e REI being sent as back-up, the counter-attack could have ended in disaster for the French forces. At Phum Preav on 16 January, the Legionnaires of this unit fought for eight hours straight to push back the Thais. The 5e REI lost its two commanding officers and 33 Legionnaires who were either killed or wounded.

A small victory for French forces occurred on the same day, but this time it was at sea. During the Battle of Koh Chang fought on 16–

The latter was the scene of the heaviest fighting and on the road that linked Phnom Penh to Saigon, the Thai advance was repulsed by the Cambodian Tirailleurs (riflemen). On 16 January 1941, a French counter-attack was launched against the main Thai column with the two sides meeting at Yang Dam Koum (Battambang) with the French attacking Thai forces around RC1, the Annam-Laos Brigade fighting against opposing forces on islands dotting the Mekong

The IJA used Indochina as a base for the invasion of the Dutch East Indies. (Author's collection)

A Vought V-93S Corsair pictured in 1945. The RTAF received its first batch of V-93Ss and V-93SAs in 1934. Known as the BJ.1 in Thai service, the V-93S was made on licence in Thailand from 1936 by the Aeronautical department at Bang sue. The V-93S was powered by a Pratt & Whitney Hornet R-1690D engine, an export version for Thailand.[7] (Photo: Service Historique de l'Armée de l'Air)

The Mitsubishi Ki-21 was a Japanese heavy bomber first produced in 1938 and used by the RTAF in the border war with France. (Author's collection)

17 January 1941, what was left of the *Marine Indochine* and its Loire 130s, attacked Thai vessels anchored near the Koh Chang Islands off the coast of southern Thailand. The two-hour battle saw the Thai navy crippled and 36 of its sailors killed.

In the skies above Indochina, on 24 and 28 January 1941, the RTAF sent nine Ki-30s, four Curtiss IIIs, and three Martin 139s, escorted by three more Curtiss Hawks, on a mission to bomb the French base at Angkor near Siem Reap airfield. The target was the largest airfield in Southeast Asia at the time, vital to French defences, and the attack was to be the last carried out in the Franco-Thai War of 1940–1941. The conflict ended after mediation by the Japanese and Vichy France was forced to cede almost all the territories it had taken from Thailand as France extended its empire towards the end of the nineteenth century.[8]

Peace negotiations started in Tokyo on 7 February 1941 with peace accords signed in Tokyo on 9 May of that year. Here, France agreed to give back to Thailand, north-western Cambodia and two Laotian enclaves. Although France regained control of these territories on 28 October 1946, at the time, the loss of nearly 70,000 sq.kms of its Asian empire dealt a severe blow to France's future colonial ambitions in the region. On the other hand, Thailand was able to celebrate victory over a European nation by constructing the Victory Monument in Bangkok in June 1941.

As the Thai authorities were soon to find out, it was Japan – not Thailand – that was to benefit the most from the Franco-Thai peace treaty. After May 1941, Hirohito gained access to Thai naval bases on the Indian Ocean and therefore, the ability to use Thailand as a corridor for attacks on the British-controlled Malaysia and Burma. The treaty also meant that Japan was now able to exploit Indochina's natural resources to support its war efforts so in the summer of 1941, it argued that it should be allowed to station military forces in the country to ward off potential attacks by foreign foes. The matter was resolved on 29 July 1941 through the signing of the Darlan-Kato agreement signed in the French city of Vichy, the home of Marshal

Twenty-four Mitsubishi Ki-30 Nagoya light bombers were supplied to the RTAF in November 1940. It was a single-engine, mid-wing, cantilever monoplane with a fixed tailwheel undercarriage and a long transparent cockpit canopy. (Author's collection)

Petain's government. It gave Japan access to eight airfields across Indochina and the IJA was permitted to base up to 40,000 troops in different areas of the country.

If it can be said that the signing of the agreement was a means of stopping Hirohito from taking complete control of Indochina, of turning the country over to the Vietnamese, or the possible internment of nearly 40,000 French nationals still in Indochina, it should also be stated that Vichy France fully supported Japan's war effort. Moreover, Decoux avidly obeyed Vichy's antisemitic policies by 'cleansing' its military in Indochina of Jews and actively pursuing anyone suspected of providing assistance to Japan's enemies, including Charles de Gaulle's Free France.

For Japan, the importance of being able to base naval forces in Indochina and Thailand had become crucial as early as July 1940 when the United States placed an embargo on all exports of oil and steel to the country. Forced to seek out other sources of war

Japanese propaganda poster during the Second World War cheering the cooperation of Asian people against Western imperialism. (Albert Grandolini Collection)

materials around the South China Sea and beyond, Japan (assisted by Vichy France) took decisive measures on 7 December 1941 when the Imperial Japanese Air Force (IJAF) and the Imperial Japanese Navy Air Force (IJNAF) launched attacks from bases in Indochina and elsewhere on US naval installations at Pearl Harbour in Hawaii and the Philippines.

The next day, the Japanese Navy attacked British forces in Hong Kong and Malaya and invaded Thailand. On 10 December 1941, the IJNAF forces based in Saigon attacked and sank two major British

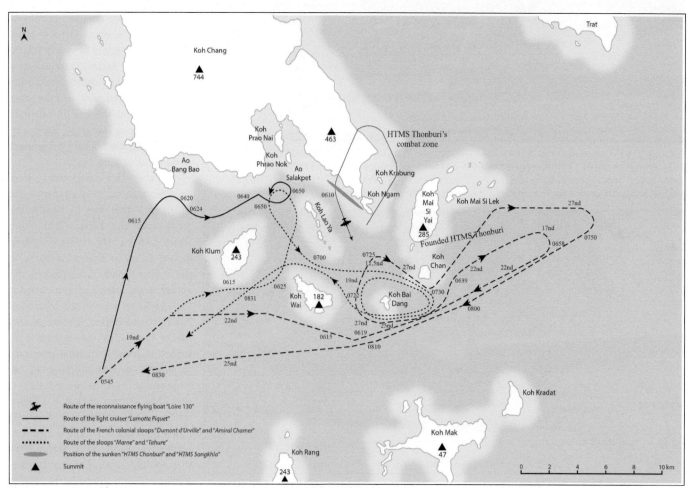

A map of the Battle of Koh Chang, fought on 16–17 January 1941. (Map by George Anderson)

Table 2		
Governor-General of Indochina and Commander-in-Chief	Vice Admiral Jean Decoux	
Senior Commander of troops in Indochina	General Maurice Martin	
Chief of Staff	Lieutenant-Colonel Marcel Alessandri	
Commander of the Artillery	General Gaston Blanc	
Division du Tonkin (DT)	Hanoi, Lang Son, Luang Prabang	
Commander-in-Chief	General Henri Cazin	
Chief of Staff	Lieutenant Colonel Lapierre	
Commander of the Artillery	General Joseph Borély	
Commander of the Artillery (1e Division du Tonkin)	Colonel Béjard	
Commander of the Artillery (2e Division du Tonkin)	General Jean Charbonneau	
Commander of the Artillery (3e Division du Tonkin)	General Fernand Rabut	
A) Hanoi Region		
9e Régiment d'Infanterie Coloniale (9e RIC)	three battalions	
2/4e Régiment d'Artillerie Coloniale (2/4e RIC)	armed with 12 x 75mm field guns and 4 x 47mm anti-tank cannons	
3/4e Régiment d'Artillerie Coloniale (3/4e RAC)	armed with 8 x 105mm Schneider howitzers and 4 x 47mm anti-tank cannons	
Détachement Motorisé du Tonkin (DMT)	nominal company of light tanks (unclear if existent), platoon of armoured reconnaissance vehicles, platoon of motorcyclists, and one transport platoon	
B) Chinese border		
5e Régiment Etranger d'Infanterie (5e REI)	three battalions.	
Bataillon Etranger d'Artillerie Légère (BEAL)	12 x 75mm field guns	
Détachement Motorisé de la Légion (DML)	AFV's as DMT (see above)	
Bataillon Laotien d'Infanterie de Montagne (BLIM)	Based at Luang Prabang and Vientiane, supported by two platoons of reconnaissance vehicles (4 Berliet VUDB armoured cars each)	
Two Compagnies Régionales de Défense (CRD)	Recruited from people living in the mountainous regions of Laos and deployed along border with Thailand)	
One armoured train based in Hanoi. Responsible for guarding the line between Hanoi and Kunming. Armed with 105mm howitzers	Armed with 105mm howitzers, 75 and 37mm cannons	
C) Brigade d'Annam	Laos (BAL)	Hué and Da Nang including divisional HQ for Pleiku.
Commander	General François Bordeau	
10e Régiment Mixte d'Infanterie Coloniale (10e RMIC)	three battalions including locally recruited troops	
2e Régiment de Tirailleurs Annamites (2e RTA)	4 battalions	
4e and 5e Bataillons Annamites d'Infanterie de Montagne (BAIM)	made up of men from tribal groups from the central Annam province based at Pleiku and Kontum	
1/4e Régiment d'Artillerie Coloniale (1/4e RIC)	armed with 16 x 75mm field guns	
Détachement Motorisé d'Annam (DMA)	nominal company of light tanks (unclear if existent), platoon of armoured reconnaissance vehicles, platoon of motorcyclists, and one transport platoon	
D) Cochinchina	Division Cochinchine	Cambodge (DCC)
Commander	General Jean de Rendiger	
Chief of Staff	Lieutenant Colonel Joseph Magnan	
Infantry Commander	General Yves de Boisboissel	
5e Régiment d'Artillerie Coloniale (5e RAC)	using 65, 75 and 105mm Schneider mountain guns	

Continued on page 14

Table 2 (continued)	
11e *Régiment d'Infanterie Coloniale* (11e RIC)	four battalions
1e *Régiment de Tirailleurs Cambodgiens* (1e RTC)	four battalions
1e *Régiment de Tirailleurs Annamites* (1e RTA)	four battalions
Détachement Motorisé de Cochinchine (DMC)	nominal company of light tanks (unclear if existent), platoon of armoured reconnaissance vehicles, platoon of motorcyclists, and one transport platoon

E) Riverine Forces:	
1. Gunboats:	
***Francis Garnier* (639 t.)**	Armaments: 2 x 100mm, 1 x 75mm, 2 x 37mm, 2 x 13.2mm, 4 x 8mm
***Argus* and the *Vigiliante* (218 t.)**	Armaments: 2 x 75mm, 2 x 37mm, 4 x 8mm, 1 x 81mm mortar
***Mytho* and the *Tourane* (95 t.)**	Armaments: 1 x 75mm, 1 x 47mm, 2 x 8mm, 1 x 60mm mortar
The *Commandant Bourdais* and the *Avalanche*: **These were two 130 t. former submarine hunters constructed in 1920 and converted to river gunboats with a total crew of 31 men.**	Armaments: 2 x 75mm, 2 x 8mm
2. Other vessels:	
***Tahure*:** **First World War Arras/Amiens-class sloop (850 t.)**	Armaments: 2 x 138.6mm, 2 x 76mm
***Marne*:** **First World War Somme-class sloop (570 t.).**	Armaments: 4 x 100mm cannons, 2 x 65mm cannons
***La Pérouse*, the *Octant*, the *Astrolabe*:** **Former survey vessels converted to dredgers.**	Armaments: La Pérouse 1 x 75mm, others 1 x 47mm
***Armand Rousseau*, the *Capitaine Coulon*, the *Paul Bert*: requisitioned and refitted vessels intended for inspections and dredging.**	
A variety of sampans, junks, small transport vessels, some equipped with a 60mm mortar or machine guns.	
Four Fairmile Type B motor boats	
3. Troops:	
3e *Régiment de Fusiliers-Marins* (RFM)	Three battalions. Total number of men: 68,000 of which 50,000 were colonial troops.

Other Naval Forces (excluding rivers):
***L'Escadre de Mer de Chine* ('China Sea Squadron') based in Cam Ranh was made up of two heavy cruisers (*Duquesne* and *Tourville*), three light cruisers (*Dugay-Trouin, Lamotte-Picquet, Primaguet*), four Chacal-class destroyers (*Léopard, Lynx, Panthère, Tigre*), and four updated Bourrasque-class destroyers (*Mistral, Tempête, Tornade, Trombe*).**

warships, battlecruiser HMS *Repulse* and battleship HMS *Prince of Wales*. Other examples of Vichy France cooperating militarily with Japan were the sending of French engineers to the Dutch Indies to help repair sabotaged oil facilities and providing intelligence on the movements of Nationalist Chinese forces and those of Claire Chennault's 'Flying Tigers', the anti-Japanese force made up of American flyers.

In fact, French AdA batteries were ordered to shoot down any Chinese or US aircraft crossing the border into Indochina. A final example of Franco-Japanese mutual assistance came when Decoux encouraged cooperation between the two countries forces to invade the French territory of New Caledonia – a collection of islands lying to the east of Australia that had declared itself supporters of Free France.[9] As New Caledonia was also a critical stop on the supply routes to Australia, Japan agreed to provide air support should Australia react. The plan was dropped at the end of the month as not enough ships could be supplied. From that moment, New

Caledonia would be defended by the United States using Task Force 6814, a force hastily brought together to defend Australia and other territories in the South Pacific.

France prepares its return to Indochina

The fortunes of the Vichy government began to turn sour with the surrender of its army during Operation Torch in French North Africa on 8 November 1942. Free French forces were taking part in the subsequent fighting to clear the rest of north and west Africa and their commander (General Henri Giraud) and de Gaulle were invited to the Casablanca Conference in January 1943. Though neither played a decisive role in determining allied strategy for the next phase of operations, their attendance at the meetings in Morocco consolidated the existence of two separate French governments and the desire for one government based abroad to liberate France.

Former Vichy French forces were welcomed back into the fold and by 3 June 1943, the French Committee of National Liberation

Members of the contingent of French soldiers attached to Force 136. These men were parachuted into Japanese-occupied Indochina to mount resistance and to gather intelligence. (Author's collection)

Paratroopers of the CLI-5 RIC, as seen during their training, in front of a C-47 Dakota transport. (Albert Grandolini Collection)

Japanese forces advance during Operation Bright Moon, March 1945. (Author's collection)

Central de Renseignements et d'Actions (BCRA) – extending the geographical scope of its cooperation with the British Special Operations Executive (SOE) from Europe to Southeast Asia.

Effectively, while Operation Jedburgh saw small teams of French, British, and Americans inserted into occupied France (and Belgium and the Netherlands) to organise local resistance from June 1944, in July, 60 men of the CLI joined up with the SOE's Force 136 based in Kandy, Ceylon. Borrowing the name of a water buffalo found in India, the guar, their role was to prepare the ground for the arrival of the remainder of the CLI.

Despite the Japanese invasion of Indochina on 9 March 1945 putting paid to the latter phase of operations, the 'guars' carried out a series of attacks on Japanese installations in northern Indochina and Laos. They also provided the intelligence for the US bombing raids on Saigon on 12 January 1945 and provided shelter for US airmen shot down during the mission.[11]

The capitulation of Vichy France as the Allies rolled through France from June 1944, came as another blow to Japan's ambitions in Asia. Japanese forces had already been pushed back in the Pacific, they were on the retreat in Burma and in Indochina, authorities formerly representing Vichy France switched allegiance to the Provisional Government of the French Republic in August 1944. Not only did this chain of events mean that Japan's sphere of influence was rapidly diminishing but it also meant that, potentially, its own forces could come under attack from a larger enemy force within a territory under its control. Indeed, its 38th Army was outnumbered by an enemy force that had previously been an ally of the IJA.

As a reaction to events in Europe and in Asia and to consolidate its positions, Operation *Bright Moon* saw the IJA invade Indochina. Japanese planners were mindful of the need to provide reinforcements

(CFLN) had been formed. Although its immediate concern was the liberation of France from Nazi Germany, attention shortly turned to the position of French colonies in a post-war context. French Indochina playing a central role in these considerations due to its size and location, the *Comité d'Action pour l'Indochine* was created just three months later. By December 1943, the committee had prepared a plan setting out how Indochina was to be taken back from the Japanese and what type of relations France would have with Indochina once it was liberated.

From a military point of view, how France would demonstrate its resistance to Japan's occupation of its colony began a month earlier when a 500-man unit named the *corps léger d'intervention* (CLI) was assembled in Djidjelli, in French Algeria. This unit formed part of the larger, battalion-sized *Forces Expéditionnaires Françaises en Extrême-Orient* (FEFEO) commanded by Lieutenant-General Roger Blaizot.[10] The plan was for the CLI to be sent to Poona in India to receive training in jungle warfare from the British so that commando operations could be carried out behind Japanese lines. Another part of the plan consisted of the French secret service – the *Bureau*

French forces captured at Lang Son, March 1945. Their commander was General Emile Lemonnier who was beheaded after refusing to surrender at Lang Son. (Author's collection)

after initial attacks were made on French forces on 9 March 1945. In the coming months, it drafted in up to 25,000 Japanese soldiers from the war theatres in China, Thailand and Burma.

The IJA faced fierce resistance from French forces in Saigon, Hanoi, Vientiane or Phnom Penh but it was, nonetheless, able to seize control of these important urban areas. It did so showing no mercy to French soldiers and one particularly brutal episode of the invasion saw the commander of French forces at Fort Brière de l'Isle near Lang Son, beheaded. Many others suffered the same fate under the orders of General Naguno on 12 March 1945, while more were machine-gunned or bayoneted to death. In all, some 544 Europeans were killed at Lang Son. To add insult to injury, the Tonkinese who survived and were taken prisoner, were formed into a column and

led away from the fort. The column was then bombed and strafed by US aircraft of the Fourteenth Air Force sent to support the French and which had mistaken the Tonkin soldiers for Japanese. Some 400–600 Tonkinese were killed during this attack.

The coming weeks proved to be a particularly tumultuous period for French civilians caught up in exactions carried out by the Japanese, for the internal politics of Vietnam and for the Japanese themselves. Effectively, Japan sought to tighten its control by using its military police, the *Kenpeitai*, to implement a brutal repression of any sign of resistance. On 11 March 1945, Japan installed Emperor Bao Dai to head a short-lived puppet regime, the Empire of Vietnam and on his arrival, he declared that through the annulation of the 1884 Treaty of Hué, or Protectorate Treaty, Vietnam was breaking all ties with France.

By mid-May, Cambodia and Laos had also declared their independence leaving the Indochinese Union in tatters. Japan's allies in Europe surrendered on 8 May 1945 leaving it as the sole Axis power and Hirohito's position was further weakened through the Potsdam Declaration made in July 1945. The declaration presented him with the choice to surrender or to face annihilation. Japanese silence in response to the ultimatum resulted in the bombing of Hiroshima and Nagasaki on 6 and 9 August, respectively. The final turning point for Japan came when the USSR declared war.

2
FRANCE RETURNS TO INDOCHINA

Britain's War in Vietnam

If France had shown that it was prepared to commit up to 60,000 troops plus naval power to South East Asia to fight the Japanese in July 1945,[1] opposition to an immediate French return to Indochina came from both the USA and the USSR. Effectively, Truman was opposed to the idea of colonialism and supported the tenets of self-determination, while Stalin expressed concerns over Vichy France's collaboration with Nazi Germany. In the end, decisions taken at Potsdam in July-August 1945 would determine just who would administer Indochina after Japan's surrender. The responsibility was handed to Lord Louis Mountbatten, the Commander of South East Asia Command (SEAC). Besides any opposition, France did not possess the logistical capacity to transport tens of thousands of troops from the mainland to its colony.

While it was fortunate for France that Mountbatten fully supported France's return to Indochina, the latter's brief was the 'reoccupation of key areas of occupied territories in order to secure effective control and to enforce surrender and disarmament of Japanese Armed Forces'.[2] To carry out his mission, he set up two organisations both headed by Major-General Douglas Gracey. The first was the Control Commission No. 1 (SACSEA) that was to use the resources of the SEAC and the second, was the Allied Land Forces French Indochina (ALFFIC), a more substantial body comprising British and French military units that reported to Headquarters Allied Land Forces South East Asia (ALFSEA) commanded by Field Marshal William Slim.

Until British and French forces arrived in Indochina in early September 1945, the Japanese were bound to act in accordance with a directive by President Truman entitled 'Instruments for the

Viet Minh troops entering Hanoi, in September 1945. (Albert Grandolini Collection)

The first Viet Minh coalition government, with Ho Chi Minh in the centre of the front row. (Albert Grandolini Collection)

Surrender of Japan: General Order No. 1.' issued on 15 August 1945.[3] Of immediate importance was the order for Japanese police forces to maintain law and order until the British and French arrived and of particular importance to the French, was that the that the Japanese should 'deliver intact, and in safe and good condition, all weapons and equipment at such time and places as may be prescribed by Allied commanders'.

Equally important to France was a document drawn up by the SEAC Joint Planning Staff entitled 'Force Plan 1: Occupation of French Indo-China' issued on 31 August 1945.[4] It stated that the eventual reoccupation of French Indochina was a matter for the French, a statement that was to dictate the conduct of the whole operation.[5] As for the operation itself, ALFSEA Operational Directive No. 12 of 28 August 1945, specified that it was to be codenamed 'Masterdom'.[6] It was to consist of two phases: the first, the British occupation, and the second, the takeover by the French.

Which British forces were to be used for the first phase had been decided upon as early as 23 August 1945 in the ALFSEA Operational Directive No. 8.[7] Its contents were forwarded to Gracey, the commander of the 20th Infantry Division, 80th Indian Brigade Indian that would make up Great Britain's first contingent of troops. Following in the footsteps of a medical team that arrived on 8 September 1945, on 11 September two companies of 1/1 Gurkha Rifles plus two companies of 1/19 Hyderabad Regiment, were dropped at Tan Son Nhut airfield by aircraft of 62 Squadron RAF. Operations continued on 12 September with 1,091 men and 26 tonnes of equipment flown in. Gracey's arrival from Rangoon on 13 September 1945 coincided with another phase of Operation Masterdom, the evacuation of over 9,000 prisoners of war who were taken to Bangkok, Thailand.

As for the task facing Gracey, it became immediately apparent to him that Saigon was on the verge of anarchy. There was rising violence between the French and the Vietnamese communities; Gracey had to

Nationalist Chinese troops manning a checkpoint in Tonkin of October 1945. (Albert Grandolini Collection)

enrol and arm Japanese troops to help keep order; there was tension between the Viet Minh claiming the independence of Vietnam. In addition, the Viet Minh attempted to persuade the Japanese not to surrender but to desert with their weapons and join the struggle. Up to 2,000 Japanese troops are said to have done so before and after the arrival of British and Indian troops.

British and French forces arrive at Saigon, September 1945 (Author's collection)

General Leclerc inspects Indian troops, Saigon, September 1945 (Author's collection)

A Japanese soldier pastes the proclamation of martial law in French, English and Vietnamese, 21 September 1945. (Author's collection)

Japanese soldiers repair Tan Son Nhut airfield, September 1945. (Author's collection)

To counter the actions of the Viet Minh, Brigadier Maunsell, Chief of Staff of the Saigon Control Commission, met with representatives of the Viet Minh on 19 September. He issued a proclamation stating that all newspapers were to be banned as were the seizing of government buildings by the Viet Minh, holding public meetings, demonstrations and the carrying of weapons. The proclamation formally issued by Gracey two days later amounted to the imposition of martial law.

As it was not possible for the British/Indian soldiers to enforce the proclamation outside of Saigon and in Vietnam's most populous areas – the places where Viet Minh activity was high – the decision was made to not only rearm Japanese soldiers to maintain order where the British did not have enough manpower, but also to release around 1,500 soldiers of the 11th Regiment of Colonial Infantry held by the Japanese in the *Martin de Pallières* military barracks since 9 March. The Viet Minh demonstrated against these measures but by then, the released French soldiers and those from the recently arrived 5e RIC, had already begun to take over police commissariats, ammunition dumps, banks, hotels and the HQ of the Viet Minh. They then raised the French flag over the building – the Maison Centrale – effectively mounting a coup d'état.

Naturally, the Viet Minh reacted in a manner similar to tactics used in irregular warfare – tactics that would be used to great effect as the years went on. Making rapid attacks on small contingents of soldiers, the most brutal occurred during the night of 24/25 September when between 150 and 300 French and Eurasian civilians, including women and children, were massacred in the *Cité Herault* suburb in north Saigon. Another attack took place two days later when OSS officer Albert Dewey was killed by the Viet Minh.

Dewey was to become the first American of nearly 60,000 to die in Vietnam. Elsewhere, the Viet Minh set up roadblocks, set fire to the city's central market area and attempted to take control of Tan Son Nhut airfield.

As more attacks on British forces over the next few days were easily repelled by soldiers with experience of fighting in Burma or around the north west Frontier, the Viet Minh's intentions became further complicated when 30,000 French troops belonging to the French *Corps Expéditionnaire Français en Extrême-Orient* (CEFEO) began to arrive.

With the Viet Minh gradually turning against Gracey's forces, it was at this point that the decision was made to employ Japanese troops to secure airfields and if necessary, to take offensive action against the Viet Minh. The Japanese assisted the British especially in Saigon, but on 1 October 1945, Gracey's remit was extended to include the outer lying areas around the city where the Viet Minh had set up bases. Though it was agreed that a ceasefire would take effect in the evening of 2 October, the truce between the two sides broke down just over a week later.

On 10 October, the Viet Minh attacked a British/Indian reconnaissance party near Tan Son Nhut with the result being the 20th Indian Division and troops from the 32nd Indian Infantry Brigade were sent to clear areas the areas around Go Vap and Gia Dinh to the north of Saigon. On this occasion, the troops commanded by Brigadier E.C.J. Woodford and supported by the armoured cars of the Indian 16th Light Cavalry, forced the Viet Minh to retreat. By that time, the Royal Air Force had the No. 273 Squadron deployed in the country: a unit equipped with Supermarine Spitfire F.Mk VIII until November 1945 and then re-equipped with Spitfire F.Mk XIV. On 3 October, the unit was issued the order to attack 'hostile targets', even if it was deployed only sparingly, as and when necessary.[8]

As the last units of the 20th Indian Division arrived by 17 October 1945, it was decided that the 100th Indian Brigade (1/1 Gurkha Rifles, 4/10 Gurkha Rifles, 14/13 Frontier Force Rifles, 16th Light Cavalry), commanded by Brigadier C.H.B. Rodham, would be sent to the areas north-east of Saigon to extinguish any sign of Viet Minh activity. This force, bolstered by Japanese troops who were responsible for the more static aspects of implementing defensive measures, was used in a more mobile capacity to counter enemy attacks and to unblock roads.

These mobile units proved to be extremely effective as the following example shows: on 29 October, Major L.D. Gates assembled a force using sections of the 16th Cavalry, the 14/13th Rifles, a detachment of Royal Engineers plus Japanese troops to capture (and kill if necessary), 2,000 Viet Minh in the area around Bien Hoa. This strategy known as GATEFORCE – a large force would set up camp from where patrols were carried out and when a

Pilots of No. 273 Squadron, RAF, as seen in front of one of their Spitfires at Tan Son Nut, in late 1945. (Albert Grandolini Collection)

The Japanese surrender was greeted by sub-lieutenant Anthony Martin of the Royal Navy (Author's collection)

for the end of January 1946 with the 20th Division due to be sent to British Borneo or other areas designated by SEAC.

While methods learnt in Burma enabled the 32nd, the 80th and the100th Brigades to hold off further attempts by the Viet Minh to capture strategic points around Saigon, by 11 January 1946, the 80th Brigade had been stood down and 12 January saw the departure of the 16th Cavalry and its armoured vehicles. The 9/12 and 2/8 Punjab regiments remained to guard Japanese soldiers at Cap St. Jacques and to oversee their repatriation but the efforts of Gracey and the 20th Division, can be seen as a resounding success in one of the most contentious situations of the immediate post-war period. Indeed, by the time the 20th Division began to leave en masse in January and February 1946, it was estimated that over 2,000 Viet Minh had been killed since the division's arrival in September 1945.

The Arrival of French Forces, September 1945

As earlier mentioned in this volume, by August 1944, France had begun to assemble military forces with a view to returning to Indochina as soon as Japan had been defeated. Plans for a return had advanced significantly by April 1945 and by 7 June that year, French General Staff had put together the fundaments of the CEFEO with General Philippe Leclerc (de Hauteclocque) as its C-in-C. Initially, the CEFEO was to be made up of two large compositions known as the 1e and 2e *Divisions d'Infanterie Colonial d'Extrême-Orient* (DICEO) made up of 26,000 men each.

However, very soon, the aforementioned transport issues put pay to these plans and they were shelved while logistical questions were resolved. A second problem confronting military planners was that many of the units of France's armed forces had been assembled

village suspected of harbouring Viet Minh was found, it was burnt down with any weapons and supplies intended for the Viet Minh, destroyed.

The methods proved to be very effective and stopped the Viet Minh in their tracks as they realised there was no hiding place. The GATEFORCE operations proved to be very successful and resulted in the death of over 200 enemy soldiers and was a method subsequently employed over the coming decades.

The arrival in November of more elements of the CEFEO and of Vice Admiral Georges Thierry d'Argenlieu as French High Commissioner, was a sign that the second phase of Operation Masterdom had commenced. The 20th Division was still used to fend off Viet Minh attempts to seize key areas of Saigon but gradually, French forces began to engage the Viet Minh using the firepower at its disposal. Gracey's troops were then able to focus on the task of enforcing Japan's surrender.

The change of guard between the British and French took place in late November as Mountbatten accepted General Terauchi Hisaichi's formal surrender. This coincided with Mountbatten and Gracey meeting General Philippe Leclerc de Hauteclocque to discuss the transfer of the military control of FIC from the 20th Division to the CEFEO. A full withdrawal of British/Indian troops was programmed

The insignia of the Corps Expéditionnaire Française d'Extrême-Orient (CEFEO). (Author's collection)

The French Army called for men to volunteer for service in Indochina. This poster for the then FEFEO proclaims 'Yesterday Strasbourg, Tomorrow Saigon. Join Up'. (Author's collection)

The *Groupement Massu* arrives in Saigon, 12 September 1945 (Author's collection)

General Leclerc and General Gracey meet in Saigon, September 1945. (Author's collection)

Leclerc inspecting British troops in Saigon, September 1945 (Author's collection)

merely for the duration of the war. Once the war had finished, the men who fought within them no longer had any obligation to remain in service and were free to return to civilian life.

Therefore, the summer of 1945 saw the general staff launch an appeal for volunteers to go to Indochina by informing them that the war against the Japanese continued in Southeast Asia and that French honour was at stake. The appeal received a favourable response and many men decided to stay on, but still the numbers could not be made up. Subsequently, it was decided that the 1e DICEO would be replaced by the 3e *Division d'Infanterie Coloniale* (3e DIC) and the 2e DICEO would be replaced by the 9e *Division d'Infanterie Coloniale* (9e DIC).

The two divisions were joined by a battle group made up of components from one of the French Army's most celebrated

armoured divisions, the 2e *Division Blindée* (2e DB). The division was commanded by Leclerc and saw action during the liberation of Paris in August 1944 but in August 1945, command was handed over to the then Lieutenant-Colonel Jacques Massu. Consequently, the group became known as the *Groupement Massu*.

In addition, France's general staff expected troops either interned by the Japanese or escaped to China, to join up with the forces it could muster. These included the 5,000 men taken by the Japanese to China after the invasion of March 1945 plus another 1,000 or so held prisoner by the Japanese in Saigon. In total, the number of French troops due to make up the CEFEO amounted to 55,000 plus another 10,000 potential recruits among the French residents of Indochina.[9] As well as French Army units, the French Navy and French Air Force began to deploy their respective forces.

Senegalese Tirailleurs present arms in Indochina. Despite the name, these regiments comprised soldiers from all of France's African colonies in French West Africa. The first regiment was created in 1857, and Senegalese Tirailleurs served in a number of wars including the First World War and the Second World War. As many as 30,000 Senegalese Tirailleurs were killed in the First World War. (Author's collection)

French troops of the 2nd Armoured Brigade (2e DB), Saigon, September 1945 (Author's collection)

French Army and Navy Forces, Order of Battle, September 1945 – February 1946

Author's notes: Information may be incomplete, and exact dates of arrival may vary.

French Army
12 September 1945

Corps Léger d'Intervention (CLI)/5e Régiment d'Infanterie Coloniale (5e RIC).

To avoid confusion with the Ceylon Light Infantry, in July 1945 the CLI was renamed the 5e RIC.

Employed as the advance guard of the CEFEO but under the orders of the SEAC and assigned to Gracey's 20th Infantry Division, 150 men of the CLI/5e RIC were transported from Algeria to India before arriving in Saigon in early September 1945. The regiment contained 6 sub-elements: the *Commando Léger 1*, the *CommandoLléger 2*, the *Commando Conus*, two autonomous units known as *Compagnies A and B*, plus a unit of naval infantrymen who had undergone parachute and commando training similar to that given to the British Special Air Service. Known, consequently, as the *Bataillon SAS*, this unit was also known as the *Commando*

Ponchardier as French admiral, Pierre Ponchardier, was the unit's first commanding officer. The unit was disbanded in September 1946 when it became part of the *Commando Hubert*.

21 September 1945

1,400 men of the 11e *Régiment d'Infanterie Coloniale* (11e RIC) held prisoner by the Japanese. Previously, and after, called 11e *Régiment d'Infanterie de Marine* (1890–1900 and 1958–1962), this regiment was based in Saigon. Battle honours: Sebastopol (1854–1855), Cochinchina (1860), Tuyên Quang (1885), Dahomey (Benin) (1893), Tien-Tsin (1900), Peking (1900), Indochina (1945, 1950, 1954), Algeria (1952–1962). Wars fought: Tonkin Expedition, Boxer Wars, Indochina War, Algerian War.

02 October 1945

Other companies of the *Commando Ponchardier* and the remainder of the CLI/ 5e RIC carried by the French warship *Richelieu* arrived at Cap St. Jacques (Vung To).

22 October 1945

2e *Division Blindée* (2e DB) known as *Groupement Massu* (GM) comprising 1,500 and organised into three sub-elements: *Sarazac*, *Grall*, and *Compagnon*. Battle honours: Invasion of Normandy (June 1944), Liberation of Paris (August 1944), Battle of Dompaire (September 1944, Liberation of Strasbourg (November 1944), Colmar Pocket (November 1944–February 1945), Western Allied Invasion of Germany (1945). Composition of advance party: 7e *Escadron*/1er *Régiment de Marche de Saphis Marocains* (RMSM) using M8 Greyhound AFVs; a squadron of the *1ère Compagnie/501ème Régiment de Chars de Combat* using the Light Tank M5A1 Stuart; a provisional infantry force drawn from the 4e *Bataillon de Marche du Tchad* (BMT); elements of the French Navy's *Régiment Blindé de Fusiliers-Marins* (RBFM); and a squad of engineers from the 71e *Bataillon du Génie*. Disbanded October 1946.

October – November 1945

9e *Régiment de Dragons*, later *Groupement d'Unités d'Armes Lourdes* (GUAL). The regiment was transported to Indochina from Bordeaux aboard the French vessels *Suffre*, *Gloire*, *Ville de Strasbourg* and *Béarn*.

December 1945

9e *Division d'Infanterie Coloniale* (9e DIC), commanded by General Jean Etienne Valluy. The division was made up by the following: the *Régiment d'Artillerie Coloniale du Maroc* (RACM); 6e *Régiment d'Infanterie Coloniale* (6e RIC) formed by members of the 4e *Régiment de Tirailleurs Sénégalais* (4e RTS); 21e *Régiment d'Infanterie Coloniale* (21e RIC) formed by members of the 6e *Régiment de Tirailleurs Sénégalais* (6e RTS); 23e *Régiment d'Infanterie Coloniale* (23e RIC) formed by members of the 13e *Régiment de Tirailleurs Sénégalais* (13e RTS); the *Régiment d'Infanterie Coloniale du Maroc* (RICM), a light cavalry regiment and the most decorated regiment of the French Army. 26e *Groupement de Forces Terrestres Antiaériennes* (26e GFTA); 71/84ème *Compagnie Mixte de Transmissions* (71/84e CMT); the 71e *Bataillon du Génie* (71e BG); 25e *Bataillon médical* (25e BM); and the logistics train.

December 1945

Brigade d'Extrême-Orient (BEO) – 1,200 men.

3e *Régiment Etranger d' Infanterie* (3e REI)

January 1946

161ème *Compagnie du Génie*. This company was first put together in Madagascar from elements of the Madagascar Brigade and became the 1e *Brigade d'Extrême-Orient* (BEO) on arrival.

2e *Régiment Etranger d'Infanterie* (2e REI) and further elements of the 2e DB.

A British-made Coventry armoured car in the service of the 5e *Régiment de Cuirassiers*. Developed at the end of the Second World War, the Coventry was the result of cooperation between Daimler and the Rootes Group. This example pictured in Phnom Penh wears the insignia of the 5e RC, a reminder of the regiment's historical links to Poland. (Author's collection)

3e *Division d'Infanterie Colonial* (3e DIC) commanded by General Georges-Yves-Marie Nyo. Disbanded in September 1946. The division comprised the following: 22e *Régiment d'Infanterie Coloniale*) made up by members of the 16e *Régiment de Tirailleurs Sénégalais* (16e RTS); 43e *Régiment d'Infanterie Coloniale*); the *Groupe de Marche deLlégion Etrangère* (GMLE) and the 3e *Groupe de Marche du Tonkin*.

6 February 1946

13e *Demi-Brigade de Légion Etrangère* (13e DBLE). This unit was made up by one company from the 1er *Régiment de Chasseurs*

Parachutistes (1er RCP); one company from the 2e *Régiment de Chasseurs Parachutistes* (2ème RCP), and elements of the 25e *Division Aéroportée* (25ème DA).

3e *Bataillon de Marche d'Extrême-Orient* (3e BMEO). The 3e BMEO was created by Commandant Bouilloc in early 1946 and contained elements of what became the 1e and 2e *Divisions de Marche du Tonkin* (DMT) in 1951. The 3e BMEO consisted of the 3e *Bataillon de Marche Sénégalais d'Extrême-Orient* (BMSEO) complemented by locally recruited troops from the Sedang and Jarai, two of Vietnam's indigenous living in the country's Central Highlands. The battalion was made up of a *Compagnie de Commandement du Bataillon* (CCB) and four battalions numbered 1 to 4. Elements of the 41e *Régiment d'Artillerie Coloniale*: 41e RAC) completed the group. The company was reinforced by Cambodians and troops recruited from the Mois and Jarais indigenous groups (Montagnard peoples).

The insignia of the 5e RC. The Latin inscription translates to 'Nothing Compares'. (Author's collection)

A French soldier in Indochina stands beside a T30 Howitzer Motor Carriage produced by the American manufacturer, the White Motor Company of Cleveland, Ohio. (Author's collection)

French soldiers on the back of a GMC CCKW 353 in 1946. The gun pictured here is a Bofors 40mm cannon. (Author's collection)

The British Humber Scout Car was a particularly valued member of France's armoured vehicle fleet in Indochina. Renowned for its mobility, the Humber was mainly used for reconnaissance and liaison. A 20mm Bofors is mounted in the turret of this example. (Author's collection)

Japanese Type 89 Chi-Ro used by the *Commando Blindé du Cambodge* (Armoured Commando of Cambodia) awaiting orders in Phnom Penh in 1946. Behind are a line of Renault UE Chenillettes used as a light armoured carrier (Author's collection)

5e *Régiment de Cuirassiers* (5e RC). Reformed on 1 May 1945, the 5e RC can trace its roots back to the reorganisation of the French Army in 1791. Also known as the Royal-Pologne (Royal Polish) Regiment, from 1947 squadrons of the regiment were based in Saigon, Siem Reap (Cambodia, Tan Son Nhut, Gia Dinh and Phnom Penh.

An observation made by Gracey in a report to General Slim on 5 November 1945, gives a clear indication of how he saw the coming years in FIC. After the release of French POWs and the arrival of the CEFEO, what is known is that thousands of men were either out for revenge against their prison guards or were seeking to restore French authority over a colony more or less controlled by Japanese and Vietnamese forces since late 1940. Indeed, Gracey was to write that: 'The French troops are leaving a pretty good trail of destruction behind them, which will result in such resentment that it will become progressively more difficult for them to implement their new policy, and I am convinced, will result in guerrilla warfare, increased sabotage and arson as soon as we leave the country'.[10]

That Gracey's predictions became patently true is undeniable given the type of war the French found themselves fighting until mid-1954. It was a war for which the French were ill-prepared as they had little experience of the irregular tactics Giap was about to unleash. As a result, the first years of an eight-year-long conflict were spent more on learning about the enemy than actually fighting him.

Unit Profile: French Navy Riverine Forces

Apart from several 'colonial roads' (*Routes Colonials*), Vietnam, Tonkin, Annam and Cochinchina of 1945, possessed very few other roads that would provide access to the mountains, forests and water-bordered areas in which the Viet Minh either endeavoured to build up popular support for its cause or carried out low-level attacks on isolated administrative and military outposts. Using Vietnam's multitude of waterways was one means of reaching these remote areas given France's lack of air power in Indochina at the time. However, if large vessels could be used to navigate larger bodies of water such as the Red River in Tonkin or the Mekong in Cochinchina, no comparably sized rivers exist in Annam. The Song Ma and the Song Ca in the north, plus the Song Ba, Don Nai and Se Bang Khan in the south, were the only rivers offering some, rather limited, access.

Otherwise, Annam is crisscrossed by a network of smaller waterways that traverse narrow valleys and which flood during the rainy season of September to January. Annam's landscape in particular, posed a great deal of problems for planners but one solution was to exploit the region's geography by creating a military force capable of accessing the interior by boat.

When the 9e DIC arrived in October 1945, as seen before, it contained naval infantry unit called the *Brigade Marine*

d'Extrême-Orient (BMEO) and another known as the Commando Ponchardier. This unit, it was believed, could be transported along shallow rivers using a variety of weapons and artillery to make attacks.

October 1945 was the first time 'brown water' forces were used in the Indochina War. British and French forces launched Operation *Moussac* to rid My Tho and its environs of a reported 1,000 Viet Minh soldiers. To do so, Leclerc sent the 2e DB along the 60km that separated Saigon from its southern neighbour. Not long after setting out, armoured vehicles and troop carriers became bogged down in thick mud or were held up by having to repair sabotaged bridges. It was decided that a waterborne approach was the only option remaining so one unit named the Compagnie Merlet plus the Commando Ponchardier, were boarded on to a Landing Craft, Infantry (LCI) provided by the Royal Navy and the French sloop *Annamite*. Sailing up the Mekong towards the end of October, the riverine forces took My Tho on 25 October then captured Vinh Long and Can Tho four days later.

When Leclerc realised how successful the operations had been, he ordered *Capitaine de Frégate* (CF) François Jaubert to assemble a riverine flotilla. Two former Japanese motorised junks renamed the *Arcachonnaise* and *Lorientaise* plus a small number of armoured barges, were the first vessels used by the newly formed brown water navy.

In December 1945, the flotilla was reinforced by the purchase of Landing Craft Assault (LCA), Landing Craft Mechanised (LCM) and Landing Craft Vehicle & Personnel (LCVP) from the British. For service and maintenance, workshops were set up in Phu My in Saigon and smaller facilities were constructed at Can Tho and My Tho in January 1946.

A month later, on 15 February 1946, the two flotillas created by Jaubert were rebaptised *Flottilles Fluviales de Fusiliers-Marins* (FFFM), or Naval Infantry River Flotillas and became collectively known as the *Flottille Fluviale d'Indochine* (FFI) or the 'Indochina River Flotilla'. The first FFFM (1e FFFM) under *Capitaine de Corvette* (CC) Hébert, was subsequently sent to operate in Tonkin from 6 March 1946 and was based at Haiphong, while the second (2e FFFM) continued to operate in the south.

The BMEO was disbanded on 1 January 1947 and replaced by the *Force Amphibie de la Marine en Indochine* (FAMIC). Still comprising two units, and still based in Haiphong, the 1e *Force Amphibie du nord* (FAN) was made up of the 1st and 3rd squadrons of the 1e *Flottille Amphibie* plus elements of the *Compagnie Jaubert*. The latter was named in honour of François Jaubert who died on 28 January 1946; three days after being wounded during operations against the Viet Minh at Than Uyen in Tonkin. As for the second group, the *Force Amphibie du Sud* (FAS), it was made up of the 2e *Flottille Amphibie* containing the 2nd and 4th squadrons plus two platoons of naval infantry.

Riverine forces take part in the attack on Can Tho, 29 October 1945. (Author's collection)

The boats used by Dinassaut forces came in several different shapes and sizes. This LCM pictured on the Mekong River in February 1946 features two Oerlikon 20mm cannons, a characteristic common to riverine craft used by the French. (Author's collection)

Types of Landing Craft

- LCI. Infantry carriers with a 180-man capacity. Armed with one 75mm gun, one 40mm Bofors, two 20mm Oerlikons, two 12.7mm machine guns, two 7.62mm machine guns, and two 81mm mortars.
- LCT. Supplied by Great Britain, the LCT. Mk 4 was the largest landing craft used by the British Army. With a crew of up to 13 men, the craft was powered by Paxmann-Ricardo diesel engines generating 500 hp each. In Indochina, these craft were used to transport men, vehicles, and supplies. The craft's initial armament of two 20mm Oerlikon cannons was increased by the addition of a 40mm Bofors, three more 20mm Oerlikons, and two 81mm mortars. At 51 metres (167 ft) in length and with a width of 11.8 metres (39 ft), the craft's transport capacity was one battalion of infantry, nine medium tanks, 12 GMC trucks or 350 tonnes of material. The FAMIC also used the LCT. Mk 6. These American-built crafts were a shorter version of the British Mk 4 and were used for logistics and transport around Cochinchina and Cambodia. Powered by three Gray Marine 6-71 engines, the craft was armed with two 20mm Oerlikons, two Lewis .303 machine guns, two Bren light machine guns and one 81mm mortar. The craft had a transport capacity of five medium tanks, nine GMC trucks, or 150 tonnes of material.
- LCA. The primary purpose of the LCA was to take troops from transport ships to shores. The LCA was 41.5 ft (12.6 m.) in length and was generally powered by a Ford V-8 petrol engine. The LCA's top speed was 10 knots, its range was 50 – 80 miles (80 – 130km), and it could carry 36 troops or an 800-lb load.
- LCVP. Used principally as a patrol boat, this 11 metre-long craft was capable of carrying up to 10 men. Armed with one Oerlikon 20mm cannon, three 7.62 machine guns and two grenade launchers, it was gradually phased out due to the noise made by its Gray Marine 64HN9 engine.
- LCM. Mainly used for transport and patrols, this craft was powered by two Gray Marine 64HN9 engines generating 330 hp in total. Armed at the stern with a 20mm Oerlikon cannon, two 12.7 machine guns, and two rifle grenade launchers, the craft could carry up to100 men, one light tank or 16 tonnes of material.
- MFV (motorised fishing vessel). These were fishing boats converted for use as coastal patrol craft.
- Harbour Defence Motor Launches (HDML), VPs (*Vedettes de Port*). These craft were used to great effect on rivers as lone patrol boats or as escorts. With a crew of eight, the craft was typically armed with two 20mm Oerlikons, two 12.7mm machine guns, and one 60mm mortar.
- Armoured barges. Initially intended to transport grain, the barges named *Dévastation*, *Foudre*, *Lave*, *Tonnante*, *Volcan*, and *Terreur* were converted to provide support for river patrols and landing operations. Typical weaponry included two Hotchkiss 13.2mm machine guns, two Hotchkiss 8mm machine guns, two Lewis .303 machine guns, plus mortars. The barges had a transport capacity of some 250 over short distances.
- Armed junks. Previously used by the Japanese, these craft were mainly use for patrol work. Typically armed with

This photo perfectly illustrates the firepower that could be delivered from landing craft, and why US naval forces in Vietnam adopted similar tactics. (Author's collection)

a 75mm field gun, one 20mm Oerlikon and a number of machine guns.
- VP (vedette de port). Tenders used for the transport of troops from ship to shore.

Composition of FAMIC, 1946–1947

FAN: 1e *Escadrille Amphibie* (based at Port-Wallut, Hong Gay, Vat Chay, Tourane)
- 3 LCIs
- 3 LCT Mk 4s
- 3 MFVs (motor fishing vessels)
- 3 HDMLs
- 2 junks

FAN: 3e *Escadrille Amphibie* (based at Hanoi, Nam Dinh, Dap Cau, Hai Duong)
- 12 LCAs
- 12 LCVPs
- 14 LCMs (Mk 3)

FAS: 2e *Escadrille Amphibie* (based at Nha Trang, Padaran, Cap St. Jacques)
- 3 LCIs
- 3 LCTs
- 8 VPs
- 3 MFVs

FAS: 4e *Escadrille Amphibie* (based at My Tho, Can Tho, Phnom Penh, Savannakhet)
- 12 LCAs
- 20 LCVPs
- 14 LCMs
- 5 armed barges
- 5 armed junks
- VPs in Cambodia and Laos

3

THE PATH TO WAR

The Characteristics of the Battlefield

To say that Indochina presented the perfect conditions in which to wage guerrilla warfare is somewhat of an understatement. In effect, from the point of view of its geography, its topography, its climate, its vegetation and its demographics, Indochina's characteristics provided Ho Chi Minh and Giap with the opportunity to play a giant game of cat-and-mouse that consisted, in the years between 1946 and 1949, of making shorts bursts of attacks on French forces then vanishing into the undergrowth, forested mountains, or back into civilian populations. As Ho said of the tactics the Viet Minh would use in these early years of the conflict and describing the fight before him, 'It is a fight between tiger and elephant. If the tiger stands his ground, the elephant will crush him with his mass. But, if he conserves his mobility, he will finally vanquish the elephant who bleeds from a multitude of cuts'.

In terms of Vietnam's natural and demographic characteristics, the two most densely populated areas are Tonkin and Cochinchina. In 1946, both had a population of some eight million people whereas Annam's population was slightly less. Hanoi, Haiphong, and Saigon were the main urban hubs, but most of the country consisted of wetlands, densely wooded mountain areas such as the Annamite Chain and the high plateaux of the Central Highlands. From here, the Viet Minh could mount attacks or take refuge from pursuing French forces. The pursuit was made more difficult by the absence, or lack of roads suitable for armoured vehicles, tanks and troops carriers – many of the dirt tracks that gave access to the interior, became swamped and impassable.

A second factor to take into account when examining the advantages for the Viet Minh and the disadvantages for the French, was the climate. For most of the year, Vietnam is under a blanket of hot and humid conditions meaning that any ground operations were mainly carried out at a snail's pace, and when the monsoon season arrived (May to October) the country was plagued with malaria-carrying mosquitos especially in and around the innumerable waterways that zigzag across Vietnam. As well as Vietnam being home to venomous snakes, such as the bamboo pit viper (or the 'two-stepper' due to its lethal venom),[1] and the King Cobra, stinging weaver ants (nicknamed 'Communist ants' by Americans due to the red colour), scorpions and spiders increased the chances of either dying or being seriously ill.

If the addition of razor sharp reeds was not enough to deal with in the hot months, winter (especially in Tonkin) brought about more misery. Snow was not an infrequent visitor to the higher areas of the region while persistent rain, not only hindered ground movements but it also impeded air transport and air support for the aforesaid. Also, French coverage of the terrain by military forces was thin. Most of the country barely saw a French soldier throughout the campaign. This guaranteed an almost free movement to Viet Minh guerrillas with an intimate knowledge of Vietnam's topography; the proximity of Laos and Cambodia also offered another escape route. It is not surprising that Giap decided to use almost unreachable areas such as these for training purposes, for supply routes and for his own troop movements to maintain the upper hand in the strategic balance.

The Breakdown in French-Viet Minh Relations, February to October 1946

In *Street Without Joy*, one of the most renowned observers of the First Indochina War, the Austrian-born Bernard B. Fall provides a strikingly accurate and concise summary of France's position in Indochina as it reassumed the responsibility of administering its colony. Writing that, 'In 1946, France seemed a likely bet for communist domination herself'– a very concise summary of the internal wranglings faced by the country – Fall also notes that the 'French forces sent to Indochina were too strong for France to resist the temptation of using them; yet not strong enough to keep the Viet Minh from trying to solve the whole political problem by throwing the French into the sea'.[2] Indeed, the events that took place between February and November 1946 consisted of the French and the Viet Minh being involved in a political struggle in which each side demonstrated that they were willing to defend and/or fight for the right to determine how Vietnam would look in the future.

The struggle began on 28 February 1946 when General Raoul Salan signed an agreement with Chiang Kai-shek in Tchoung King that saw French troops replace the Chinese National Army north of the 16th parallel. An agreement that met Ho Chi Minh's approval, on 6 March 1946 he then signed a second agreement with Special Envoy of France, Jean Sainteny.

As President of the Democratic Republic of Vietnam, Ho agreed to allow France to continue to station troops in North Vietnam. France, in turn, recognised Vietnam as a 'Free State' within a proposed 'French Union' of old and new colonies, associated states like Viet Nam and UN Trust Territories such as French Cameroons or French Togoland. The idea of a union of French-speaking nations was the brainchild of Charles de Gaulle who recognised the need for political reform if France was to remain a colonial force. As for Vietnam itself, de Gaulle's ambitions found support and opposition within the French government and with the French military: Leclerc and Sainteny opposed communism but realised that Vietnamese nationalist aspirations were valid, while others such as Colonel Henri Cedile and Admiral Georges Thierry d'Argenlieu, opposed the idea of granting Vietnam full autonomy.

As Commissioner for Cochinchina and French High Commissioner to Vietnam respectively, their view was that the agreement of 6 March only applied to North Vietnam (Tonkin) and that Cochinchina (South Vietnam), was a free state equal to other Indochinese members of the French Union, Laos, Cambodia and Tonkin. A signatory of the March agreement, French Overseas Minister Marius Moutet, confirmed that this was the case on 14 March 1946.

In order to clarify the terms of the Ho-Sainteny agreement, Ho held talks with d'Argenlieu on the French cruiser *Emile Bertin* in Ha Long Bay on 24 March. It was agreed that that the two sides would open further talks, hold diplomatic exchanges between the two countries and that preparatory meetings would take place in Da Lat before the drawing up and signing of any official agreement.

The tone used by the Vietnamese at the meetings was set by Nguyen Binh, the commander of the 7th zone of the Vietnamese National Defence Army, when he accused d'Argenlieu of not complying with the terms agreed on 6 March. He called on the Vietnamese people and the Viet Minh, to engage in a general offensive on all fronts and to sabotage all French public bodies in Cochinchina.[3] At the same time, France also showed that it was prepared to use its own military strength and political nous. On 26 March, French troops marched into Hué, the former capital of Annam and set up a provisional government for Cochinchina, headed by Nguyen Van Trinh.

Despite these accusations, calls to war, and chess-board manoeuvres, the Da Lat Conference was held on 17 April 1946. It came to nothing as the French insisted that the five Indochinese states were to be formed into an entity named the French Union of Indochina. Negotiations were then transferred to France and were held at Fontainebleau, just southeast of Paris, on 6

Ho Chi Minh during talks with French officials, Paris, 2 July 1946 (CVCE)

July 1946. They were suspended by the Vietnamese on 1 August amid reiterated accusations that the French had not respected the Ho-Sainteny agreement. This decision illustrated the political rift between Left and Right-wing positions that dominated post-war France and would heavily influence what means and support were given to French troops as they fought a war in Indochina.

In effect, while the Left-wing press found that the suspension of the talks was justified, the Right-wing press fully supported France's position. For example, the Communist *Humanité* spoke of the 'flagrant dissonance' between French statements in Paris and French policy in Indochina, while *Aurore* demanded that France should not 'abdicate' from its position in Indochina. Both the Left-wing and independent press agreed, however, that war was going to be the outcome of the failure to agree terms: the independent *Ordre* stated that the time for a showdown had come, while *Combat* on the Left, expected 'serious repercussions'.[4]

The main sticking point that caused negotiations to be suspended was France would not commit itself to a date for a referendum on the question of Vietnamese unification as stipulated on 6 March. To resolve the issue, more talks were held between Ho and French authorities in September 1946 and on 14 September, he signed a joint declaration and *modus vivendi* with Marius Moutet that provided for provisional solutions to be implemented while permanent ones could be reached.

Amongst other measures relating to education and economic freedom, the September agreement specified that all fighting in Cochinchina was to cease and that a mixed commission of general staffs

would ensure that this measure was respected.[5] A few hours after the latest agreement had been signed, Ho Chi Minh left Paris for Toulon where he boarded a ship bound for Saigon.

The Haiphong Incident, November 1946

The formalisation of the French Union and the founding of the Fourth Republic on 27 October, were confirmation of a rebirth of France both on domestic and international levels. Both most certainly strengthened France's resolve to assert itself in its overseas territories, and as for Indochina, little time was wasted showing that France and not the Viet Minh, was in the driving seat when it came to determining the country's future.

The first significant illustration of this resolve occurred on 20 November 1946 when a French vessel intercepted a Chinese junk entering the port city of Haiphong after claiming that it was attempting to bring in contraband. Though intervention appears justified, perceived political overreach on France's behalf prompted the intervention of local Vietnamese to fire on the French vessel as an expression of their anger and opposition to French moves. Soon

Haiphong burns after the French bombardment of the city on 19 December 1946. (Author's collection)

rioting had spread throughout the city leading to the deaths of 24 French soldiers with another 68 were injured.

On 22 November, the locals, now reinforced by the Viet Minh, ambushed a French burial detai,l causing the deaths of six more soldiers. The French sought to restore peace by agreeing to respect Vietnamese authority over trading rights in Haiphong, however once d'Argenlieu learnt of the deaths of French soldiers, he ordered General Jean Etienne Valluy to organise a swift riposte. In turn, Valluy ordered Colonel Pierre-Louis Debès, the commander of French forces in Haiphong, to take complete control of Haiphong and to 'give a severe lesson to those who have treacherously attacked you'.[6]

Invoking a Franco-Chinese treaty signed in February 1946 that gave the French jurisdiction to engage in combat should the need to protect the Chinese in Haiphong arise, Debès also ordered that the Vietnamese evacuate the French and Chinese quarters of the city and that the French be allowed to set up a zone of occupation. After the Viet Minh government had refused to comply with these demands, on the morning of 23 November, French naval ships *Le Chevreuil*, *Savorgnan de Brazza*, *Dumont d'Urville* and the *Suffren* began a bombardment of some of the most populous areas of Haiphong.

The French took full control of the city by 28 November and it is generally agreed, that up to 6,000 Vietnamese had died during the raid. At this point, there was no immediate military threat to Ho Chi Minh's government in Hanoi or to the rural areas of Tonkin and northern Annam that were firmly under the Viet Minh's control. However, Giap pulled all his regular battalions out of Haiphong and Hanoi and began to march them towards the Viet Bac and the South Delta Base.[7]

While some Viet Minh were also ordered to merge back into the local populations or patrol the streets of Hanoi, tensions increased on 19 December when the French high command instructed these soldiers to disarm as a sign of the Viet Minh's good intentions towards France. Giap's response was to order more barricades to be erected and to prepare an operational plan for an attack on French positions in the city. Though Giap met with General Louis Molière in an attempt to lessen the probability of a full-blown conflict, an agreement could not be met. An attack launched by Giap was easily repulsed leading to heavy Viet Minh casualties, and with this Giap made a national call to arms.[8]

On 21 December, Ho Chi Minh issued his own statement in which he set out the reasons why his only alternative was to go to war. In the statement, he accused French 'reactionary colonists' of 'lacking sincerity' and regarding the modus vivendi of 14 September, as a 'scrap of paper'. For him, the French had set up a puppet government, they had 'terrorised' his compatriots, they had invaded Vietnamese territory, and they tried to 'strangle the Vietnamese people' and 'wreck' their national sovereignty. According to Ho, the 'obvious and undeniable aim' of these French colonists was to reconquer Vietnam. For him, the 'Fatherland' was in danger and needed to be protected.[9] In the name of the government and the Vietnamese Communist Party, Ho Chi Minh then called for people everywhere to 'exterminate the enemy' and to 'fight to the last drop of blood'.[10] Thus started the First Indochina War.

The People's War

The people's war was a war for the people by the people. For the people because the war's goals are the people's goals – goals such as independence, a unified country, and the happiness of its people – and by the people: not just the army but all people.

We had to force the enemy to fight the way we wanted them to fight. We had to force the enemy to fight on unfamiliar territory.

All the conceptions born of impatience and aimed at obtaining speedy victory could only be gross errors. It was necessary to accumulate thousands of small victories to turn them into a great success.

All quotes: Vo Nguyen Giap

In many respects it was to be expected that Cochinchina was the source of anti-French activism in 1940. In 1916, activists based in this southern region of Indochina revolted and forced the intervention of the military and in their view, they were merely continuing a revolutionary legacy left behind by the Can Vuong movement, a large scale nationwide insurgency against the French that started in 1885.

Whereas both revolts failed in their objectives due to France's military ability to suppress uprisings, in 1940 the Standing Committee of the Indochinese Communist Party (ICP) believed that France's febrility presented the opportunity to implement a plan of action hatched as early as 1930 and the founding of the party. The plan based on 10 main points, among them was to 'overthrow to French imperialism, to make Indochina independent, to establish a worker-peasant-soldier government and to confiscate all businesses and property belonging to the imperialists'.[11] The Standing Committee, headed by Vo Van Tan in March 1940, had a sense that low-paid workers and peasants would support any move to oust the French given their growing dissatisfaction with inflation, an increase in unemployment and a decrease in the standard of living for most Vietnamese.

As there was widespread discontent at the decision by the French to enforce conscription,[12] it was hoped that an uprising in Cochinchina would spark a nationwide anti-French movement, as seen in the latter part of the nineteenth century. For this reason, Van Tan oversaw the provision of politically and military training for workers in factories in Saigon or in rural areas in the south, throughout the summer of 1940. In November, representatives of the ICP's Central Committee and the ICP's Regional Committee for Tonkin, met in Hanoi to discuss the possibility of implementing a generalised insurrection.

The idea met with disapproval as on 27 September, this branch of the ICP had launched its own attempt to overthrow the French at Bac Son as Japanese forces were in the process of crossing the border. On this occasion, more than 600 Vietnamese insurgents drawn from local ethnic groups (such as Tay, Dao, Nung, and Kinh) attacked Mo Nahl station in the northeast region of Lang Son and started the Bac Son revolt. Further attacks occurred against Canh Tiem and Sap Di Pass, at which point the French sent troops to suppress the revolt. This included attacks on the civilian population, an additional motivation to join any future popular revolt to oppose France.

However, at the meeting Hanoi, it was agreed that mistakes at Bac Son had been made, that the conditions needed for a successful campaign against the French were not yet in place and that renewed attempts to dislodge the French, had to be better coordinated. It was agreed, however, that the core elements of the Bac Son forces should be maintained as guerrilla units in the Viet Bac, a region north of Hanoi and the area that served as a support base for the Viet Minh as it launched operations in 1946.[13]

The misgivings presented at the Hanoi meeting of early November 1940 did not, however, dissuade the ICP in the south. In the Mekong Delta from 22 November 1940, 15,000 Vietnamese insurgents began to cut off roads, seize villages and rid them of those accused of collaboration with the French through summary executions. The period from 22–30 November was when the most intense fighting took place and as provinces around Saigon (Gia Dinh, Cho Lon, My Tho and Can Tho) fell to the insurgents, the insurrection spread rapidly to other provinces.

By then, the Vichy French authorities had initiated a reaction and had sent in the 5e *Régiment Etranger* (RE Regiment of the Foreign Legion). This force was backed by artillery and bombing raids that flattened villages so 30 November, the insurrection began to lose momentum and by the end of the year, it had almost disappeared. The lessons learnt from the failed Cochinchina uprising were, nevertheless, that the conditions for revolutionary action had to be right and that the communist forces required a much more organised and coordinated approach.

After the usual purges within organisations such as the ICP had taken place, the reorganisation of forces began at Pac Bo on the Tonkin border with China in May 1941. Here, Ho Chi Minh met with other communist cadres to decide on a plan of action. The group adopted a strategy whereby the use of guerrilla warfare and the formation and training of local populations, was central to an overall revolutionary strategy. Using Cao Bang as a base, and with Vo Nguyen Giap at his side, Ho promoted the composition of National Salvation Associations specifically in the Ha Quang, Hoa An and Nguyen Binh districts of the Cao Bang province.

The number of members of these associations grew rapidly and by May 1941, Ho was ready to expand the creation of associations on a national level. He presented his strategy at the Eighth Plenum of the Party Central Committee early that month and it was agreed that priority be given to serving the interests of the Vietnamese people, regardless of their position in society. The central tasks that lay ahead were the building of political and military forces, the forming of revolutionary bases and preparations for revolutionary activity. On 19 May 1941, the Party Central Committee decided that the name of the new organisation would be the Viet Minh Front and that its ultimate goal was national independence for Vietnam.

Who was Ho Chi Minh?

Born in 1890 in Central Vietnam, Ho Chi Minh's father, Nguyen Sinh Sac, was a Confucian scholar and later an imperial magistrate. Although this meant he was eligible to serve as a member of the imperial administration, Nguyen Sinh Sac chose not to take advantage of his position as it would mean serving the French. A form of protest at French occupation of the country that had an early effect on Ho Chi Minh, he nonetheless attended a French school in Hué that would later see the arrival of future North Vietnamese Prime Minister, Pham Van Dong, future general, Vo Nguyen Giap and future Prime Minister of South Vietnam, Ngo Dinh Diem.

Travelling to Saigon in 1911, Ho first worked as a kitchen assistant on a French vessel named the *Amiral de Latouche-Tréville*. The ship left Saigon in June 1911 and docked in Marseille a month later and from here, Ho (using the alias Van Ba) also visited Le Havre and Dunkirk before going to Marseille in September. He unsuccessfully applied to enrol at the *Ecole nationale de la France d'outre-mer* (French Colonial Administrative School) in Paris and so continued to work on the ship as it enabled him to travel.

n 1912, Ho reached the United States where he claims to have lived in New York and where he became influenced by the Pan-Africanist Marcus Garvey and attended meetings of the fledging Universal Negro Improvement Association. Other claims later made by Ho were that he worked in London at the Carlton Hotel

Ho Chi Minh and VM partisans circa 1945. (Author's collection)

under French chef Auguste Escoffier and that he worked in various catering establishments dotted around the UK capital.

What can be verified is that by 1919, Ho had returned to France and had befriended Marcel Cachin, a French Communist politician and a member of the *Parti socialiste de France* (French Socialist Party). Ho's political development continued when he joined the *Groupe des Patriotes Annamites* (Group of Vietnamese Patriots). The group published newspaper articles calling for the independence of Vietnam from the French and petitioned Western powers during the Versailles peace talks of 1919 for the recognition of the civil rights of the Vietnamese under French rule, the end of French rule in the county and the forming of a wholly independent Vietnamese government. Though the group's request were rejected by participants of the talks, including French premier Georges Clemenceau and US president Woodrow Wilson, Ho Chi Minh's role in the events established him as the public face of Vietnamese independence. His profile was further highlighted when he showed support for Bolshevism at public meetings where he would encourage French socialists to join the recently created Communist International of Vladimir Lenin.

In 1920, Ho's commitment to socialist ideals were confirmed when he was elected as a representative to the Congress of Tours of the Socialist Party of France in December of that year and it was here that he became a founding member of the French Communist Party. Ho then took up a position in the Colonial Committee of the party and again, attempted to rouse support for the people of Vietnam.

In 1923, Ho adopted the pseudonym Chen Vang and travelled from Paris to Moscow. Assuming the identity of a Chinese merchant, in Moscow Ho was employed by Comintern (the Communist International) and began studies at the Communist University of the Toilers of the East, a training school for important communist figures and those seen as having the potential to promote communism throughout the world. Its alumni included Harry Haywood, a leading figure in the Communist Party of the United States (CPUSA) and Jomo Kenyatta, the first indigenous Head of State of Kenya. The next year, Ho attended the Fifth Comintern Congress and later that year, he made his way to Guangzhou in southern China using the name Ly Thuy.

The years 1924 to 1941 saw Ho take up a variety of roles in countries such as India, Hong Kong and the Soviet Union but by 1938, Ho was acting as an adviser to the Chinese Communist armed forces of Mao Zedong. This was to be Ho Chi Minh's last role before he decided to devote his time to ridding Vietnam and Indochina of all colonial presence. When France was defeated in the spring of 1940, Ho Chi Minh, Vo Nguyen Giap and Pham Van Dong, seized the opportunity to strengthen the push for Vietnamese independence. It was around this time, that Nguyen Ai Quoc began to use the name Ho Chi Minh ('He Who Enlightens').

The French Reaction to Viet Minh Activities, 1941–1945

As for the French authorities, by mid-1941 they had begun a campaign to pacify any sign of rebellion in northern Tonkin. The result of this campaign was that by August, the Viet Minh had been forced to retreat to southern China where they sought support from the Chinese Nationalist Party, the Kuomintang (KMT) which had a long history of sponsoring various Vietnamese nationalist groups. The Chinese also set up training camps for Vietnamese nationalist forces, the presence of which was discovered by Japanese intelligence services based in Shanghai. They reported to the French that the KMT was training eight battalions of which three were assigned guerrilla operations along the Tonkin border and that around 300 men and women were being trained to maintain contact with operatives in French Indochina.[14]

With Ho Chi Minh arrested and imprisoned by the Chinese in August 1942 due to suspicions surrounding his communist activities, throughout 1943, French authorities continued to seek out Viet Minh activists and suppress all forms of anti-French sentiment from within Indochina. This included arresting several leading figures in the Red River Delta region and around Saigon when demonstrations against French rule took place in August of the same year.

Though Decoux made trips through Cochin, Annam and Tonkin in the autumn of 1943 and found no evidence of renewed Viet Minh activity, in December 1943 and February 1944, he was to report that military clashes had taken place and these encounters were precursors to an increase in the number of small-scale revolts in the Tonkin in the spring.

The summer of 1944 saw little activity but in November, a peasant rebellion broke out in Thai Nguyen and Tuyên Quang, two provinces in Tonkin. What spurred the rebellion was a shortage of food caused by mismanagement of the price of rice; itself caused by the Japanese occupation of Indochina and US desires to attack the Japanese. Indeed, in 1944, the Allies began a bombing campaign that destroyed the supply lines between Tonkin and Annam with the intention of severely reducing the amount of coal transported between Tonkin and Japanese bases in Saigon. Whereas one outcome was that northern Vietnam was unable to receive rice from Cochin and Cambodia, another was that the French and the Japanese were forced to used rice and maize to fuel power stations.

To compound an already serious shortage of the staples of the Vietnamese diet, drought and pests during the winter-spring harvest of 1944/1945 caused a decrease in rice production in northern Vietnam by some 20 percent.

Various sources put the number who died from starvation at between 400,000 and two million.

The Viet Minh took advantage by joining the peasants in the riots and demonstrations that took place towards the end of 1944. Reports stated many of the 7,000 Vietnamese that took part, were armed. The reaction of the French authorities was to send three battalions of Legionnaires supported by artillery and tanks.[15] By February 1945, the revolt in the Tonkin had run out of steam save a few isolated pockets of guerrilla fighters offering sporadic resistance. Nonetheless, if the French believed they had successfully seen out the challenge of the Viet Minh, they seriously underestimated the resourcefulness of a movement that had its eyes set on national liberation at whatever cost.

The Rise of the Viet Minh and the August Revolution of 1945

Neither the end of the Tonkin revolt, nor the Japanese invasion of March 1945, diminished the resolve of the Viet Minh. The Tonkin Revolutionary Conference of the Viet Minh took place in Hanoi from 15–20 April and called for a joint Vietnamese/Chinese plan to be put together to defeat the Japanese. Seven war zones across Vietnam were to be created to achieve the objective and information was to be spread among the Vietnamese people to explain why a violent uprising was the only option left.[16]

From that moment, the tide began to turn in the Viet Minh's favour and by May 1945, it had created a zone free of Japanese presence. The zone consisted of the provinces of Cao Bang, Bac Can, Lang Son, Ha Giang, Thai Nguyen, Phu Tho, Phuc Yen, Yen Bai and Tuyên Quang, as well as parts of Bac Giang and Vinh Yen.[17] The outcome of the rapid expansion of the Viet Minh's sphere of influence was the formal declaration of the establishment of the People's Liberation Army on 15 May, during ceremonies at the Bien Thuong Buddhist temple in Cho Chu village in the Thai Nguyen province.

The influence of the Viet Minh increased so much that by 4 June 1945, the movement controlled vast swathes of the northern region between Hanoi and Cao Bang. This enabled the Viet Minh to declare the existence of a free zone headed by a five-man executive committee including Giap, with Tan Trao named as its capital. To show that the Viet Minh meant business, one month later, Giap ordered an attack

Members of the Deer Team providing weapons training to the Viet Minh in the summer of 1945 (NARA).

Staff of the Deer Team, as seen at the start of their mission. (Albert Grandolini Collection)

Ho Chi Minh pictured with OSS operative Allison Thomas, circa July 1945. Ho Chi Minh was given the codename 'Lucius'. (NARA)

on Japanese positions in the Tam Dao mountains.[18] The positions were overrun, and any prisoners were freed. Now that the Viet Minh had established an operational base from which it could carry on its activities almost unhindered by outside interference, its ambition to control an even greater share of Vietnam received assistance from the nation that sought to obliterate the Viet Minh only two decades later.

The Viet Minh and the OSS

In a similar way to which Vietnamese Hmong tribesman were recruited by the CIA to fight the Laotian part of the Vietnam War, by early 1942 the US Office of Strategic Services (OSS) were seeking out homegrown Vietnamese movements to assist its efforts to undermine the Japanese in Indochina. Even though Indochina was under Japanese occupation and of little operational interest to the Allies, having an intelligence network in the country was particularly useful and a network of operatives inside the country provided valuable intelligence.[19]

Operatives were able to provide information on weather conditions; indications of significant Japanese troop movements (valuable for the analysis of Japanese strategy); and the same network could provide a safe haven for allied air crews shot down over northern Viet Nam. Indeed, there were many examples of rescued airmen being taken across Japanese held territory to the US Fourteenth Air Force base at Kunming in China.

What had been a steady flow of intelligence stopped suddenly with the Japanese invasion of Indochina on 9 March 1945. A new means of gathering intelligence had to be found so it was fortunate

Vo Nguyen Giap. Often described as one of history's greatest military strategists, Giap worked with the Deer Team in the summer of 1945. (Author's collection)

that an OSS man named Charles Fenn, recalled hearing of a certain Ho Chi Minh in October 1944.[20] After another OSS agent named Frankie Tan, urged Ho to work with the OSS and so Ho travelled to Kunming in April 1945 to discuss matters further. Here, Ho met Major Archimedes Patti and plans for Ho to pass on information to the United States were finalised.[21] From that moment, Ho Chi Minh became an operative of the OSS and was given the moniker 'Lucius'.[22]

As the Viet Minh gradually became considered as not just an asset but also an ally, the OSS set up a unit known as the Deer Team whose role was to attack and intercept Japanese materials transported along the railroad between Hanoi and Lang Son. On 16 July 1945, a group of six men, commanded by Major Allison Kent Thomas and including French speaker Henry Prunier, arrived by parachute at the Viet Minh headquarters at Kim Lung. Thomas had been instructed to organise another group of between 50 to 100 guerrillas and to arm them, containers of small arms and explosives were dropped in.[23]

The job of finding enough men to carry out the attacks on the Japanese and arming them, was made easier by the Viet Minh. Ho informed Thomas that he had over a thousand men ready to fight and Thomas saw that some were armed with Brens, 'tommies' (Thompson machine guns) and a few rifles captured from the French.[24] This arsenal was complemented a few days later when the US provided more Brens and Thompsons, along with M-1 carbines, M-1 rifles, Colt .45 pistols, and binoculars.

Six other members of Deer Team arrived on 29 July and set to work training the Viet Minh for operations. Among the Viet Minh present at the camp and with whom the Deer Team worked closely, was Vo Nguyen Giap. He was known to the Americans as 'Mr. Van'.[25] Early August was spent setting up a training camp, barracks to house the 110 Viet Minh recruited by the OSS, plus an infirmary and a communications centre. 40 of the recruits were selected to form the Vietnamese American Force (Bo Doi Viet-My).

Although one can speculate as to whether US assistance to the Viet Minh in some way emboldened Ho Chi Minh (Claire Lee Chennault of the Flying Tigers was a figure revered by the Viet Minh), what is known is that Ho had a habit of striking when the iron was hot and taking advantage of political shifts that had the potential of working in his favour.

Allison Thomas joins the Viet Minh as they march towards Hanoi in mid-August 1945. (NARA).

One such shift concerned the Japanese coup d'état of 9 March 1945. The French had remained the colonial masters even after the Japanese occupation of Indochina in 1941, but the coup severed the head that governed and led to Bao Dai becoming ruler of the Empire of Vietnam, an independent entity only in spirit as the Japanese held the whip hand over the power structure it had put in place. Indeed, though Bao Dai became emperor on 11 March 1945, it was not until June and July that the Japanese permitted any degree of authority to be passed on to Vietnamese prime minister, Tran Trong Kim; and not until 14 August that Bao Dai was given permission to abrogate the treaties that gave France authority over Cochinchina in 1862 and 1874.[26]

Ho Chi Minh knew that the Bao Dai government was a mere puppet of the Japanese, he knew that the Japanese had been defeated; and he knew that the control of Southeast Asia had swayed in favour of the United States. Ho also knew that the United States regarded Indochina as an extension of the China Theatre of war, that Chinese forces were due to enter Indochina north of the 16th parallel to receive Japan's surrender (as per the conditions of the Potsdam Conference) and that the British were to receive its surrender south of this line.

Lastly, Ho knew that Mountbatten was favourable to the return of Indochina to France, a situation that his political philosophy could not allow.

It being expedient that Ho activate his forces as early as possible in order to demonstrate both the legitimacy and strength of the Viet Minh movement, Ho called for a meeting of Viet Minh and other officials who gathered on 13 August to discuss what measures needed to be taken. At the end of the discussions, a National Insurrection Committee was created and its first motion, Military Order Number 1, was to declare that an insurrection start immediately.

The drawing up of a plan of action was the next item on the agenda of the committee and on 16 August, it convened the National People's Congress held in a communal house in Tan Trao in the Tuyên Quang province. The gathering involved representatives from all sectors of Vietnamese society and these representatives, known as People's Revolutionary Committees, took over the administration of villages and towns as Viet Minh forces made their way to Hanoi.

The Viet Minh took control of the city on 19 August and Ho Chi Minh's Vietnamese Provisional Government took over. The next stage in the Viet Minh's rise to power was the abdication of Bao Dai on 25 August. His abdication led to the August Revolution being declared a success that day and on 2 September 1945, Ho Chi Minh read the Proclamation of Independence to thousands of people gathered at Ba Dinh Square in Hanoi. The proclamation referred to the US Declaration of Independence, the French Declaration on the Rights of Man and the Citizen, but it made clear that France was the enemy of the Vietnamese people.

According to Ho, the 'French imperialists' had deprived the Vietnamese of every democratic liberty; they enforced inhuman laws; Vietnamese national unity had been destroyed by setting up three distinct regimes in the north, the centre, and the south of Vietnam; and the French had impoverished the Vietnamese while robbing them of mines, forests and natural resources. He went on to praise the recent creation of the United Nations Organisation (ONU): of particular relevance to Vietnam's situation was the organisation's belief that non-self-governing peoples had the right to self-determination and the freedom to take their own decisions on their futures. In regard to this tenet, Ho emphasised that the Vietnamese were 'determined to mobilise all their physical and mental strength, to sacrifice their lives and property to safeguard their independence and liberty'.[27]

An Example of a Viet Minh Operational Zone: War Zone D

The letter 'D' standing for 'Dong Nai' in southeast Vietnam, 'War Zone D', or 'War Zone RED', was the name given to the VM's area of operations in this part of the country. Created in February 1946, it was first centred around five communes (Tan Hoa, My Loc, Tan Tich, Thuong Tan and Lac An), but then came to include areas along the Vietnamese border with Cambodia. Four areas of southern Vietnam were codenamed A, B, C, and D and each area performed a different role. 'Zone A' was a communications base in Giap Lac; 'Zone B' was a logistics base located in Chang Lang; 'Zone C' was the army's operational base located in Ong Doi; and 'Zone D' was initially the HQ of Zone VII. Over time, 'Zone D' became synonymous with Zone VII and covered the provinces of Thu Dau Mot, Bien Hoa, Tay Ninh, Gia Dinh, Cholon, Ba Ria, and Saigon.

Viet Minh Organisation and Strategy

It has been well-documented that Giap was heavily influenced by the military strategies developed by Mao Tse-tung during China's war with Japan in the 1930s. Like Ho Chi Minh, Giap spent the latter part of this decade and the early 1940s, learning what he could about the tactics, strategy, equipment, training and recruitment used by China's Eighth Route Army. Officially known as the 18th Group Army of the National Revolutionary Army of the Republic of China, this unit was commanded by the Chinese Communist Party but integrated into the national Kuomintang military forces. Of all Mao's writings on the fighting of revolutionary warfare, Giap was particularly impressed with his theories on the extensive use of irregular warfare whereby a smaller, less powerful, but more mobile army, could defeat a larger army that still employed conventional, or regular, tactics.

Mao's thoughts, themselves, borrowing and adapting much earlier theories developed by Chinese military strategist Sun Tzu in *The Art of War*, his *On Guerilla Warfare* written in 1937, used examples such as the First Opium War (1839–1842), the Taiping Rebellion (1850–1864) and the Boxer Uprising (1899–1901) to construct conclusions such as, while military action and political affairs are not identical, it is impossible to isolate one from the other.

Seeing parallels in Vietnam's war with France, Giap – and Ho Chi Minh – implemented a conceptual framework also developed by Mao called the *dau tranh* strategy, an integrated political and military strategy consisting of three phases: strategically defensive; a period during which forces were built up; offensive action. Guerilla actions would be used during the first two phases while the final phase reverted to the use of conventional warfare. In contrast to Mao's theories, what can be noted from the following table, is that a more international aspect was added to form a three-pronged strategy to obtain victory.

Table 3	
Political Strategy	**Military Strategy**
Dan Van – Action amongst the people The use of organisational measures to manipulate the masses and generate fighting units. *Binh Van – Action against enemy soldiers* The use of propaganda to lower the moral of the enemy. *Dich Van – Action against the enemy's people* The use of propaganda to convince the enemy's people (French population in this case) that there was discontent and desertion in the ranks and that the war was unwinnable.	*Phase 1. Organisation and preparation* The recruitment of fighters and the stockpiling of weapons. *Phase 2. The use of guerrilla warfare* Carrying out terrorist attacks, sabotaging infrastructure, ambushing the enemy, setting up revolutionary administrative structures in captured areas, et cetera *Phase 3. The use of conventional warfare* The use of regular military formations and tactics to capture key areas.

The first steps to create an organised form of armed resistance to the French, were taken on 2 September 1945 with the establishment of the DRV and a Ministry of National Defence. Further organisational developments took place on 3 November 1946 with the founding of the Committee of National Defence (CND), or Supreme Defence Council (SDC). While Ho Chi Minh was commander-in-chief of this body, with its creation, Giap became overall commander of the People's Army of Vietnam (PAVN) created on 22 December 1944. On the next level down from Giap, were three directorates responsible for the spreading of propaganda and the indoctrination of troops and civilians (General Political Directorate led by General Nguyen Chi Thanh); the training, recruitment, and discipline of PAVN troops (General Staff Directorate led by General Hoang Van Thai); and the procurement of supplies and weapons (General Supply Directorate led by Tran Dia Nghia from December 1946). On the

Women fighters of the Viet Minh. Every Vietnamese man, woman and child was expected to make a contribution to the Viet Minh's war effort. (Author's collection)

Lieutenant-General Nguyen Binh. The speed with which French and British forces had taken control of Cochinchina from September to November 1945 led the Viet Minh Central Committee (*Trung uong*) into sending war-hardened revolutionary Lieutenant Nguyen Binh to establish Viet Minh resistance. Setting up base in the Plain of Reeds near Saigon, Binh began to unify local anti-French bandit groups or religious sects into a United National Front (*Mat Tran Quoc Gia Lien Hiep*) that was willing and able to take on counterattacks against enemy forces. In December 1945, Binh was then appointed commander of the whole of the ICP's War Zone VII (*Bo Tu Lenh Khu VII*) of Dong Nam Bo (southeast Vietnam) that included Saigon. Binh recognised the need to avoid direct confrontation with French forces, so he focused his efforts on breaking up larger units of Viet Minh and creating smaller, company-sized, units known as *Chi Doi*. These units were responsible for carrying out small operations such as ambushes against small or weaker French patrols outside Saigon. Inside Saigon, Binh also attempted to disrupt daily life by recruiting locals to carry out the assassination of Vietnamese administrative officials working for the French. (Author's collection)

Often encountered in rice paddies and areas where they could be easily concealed were barbed spikes set in wood or concrete. To make any injury worse, human excrement could be smeared on the tip of the spikes. Another interesting aspect of this photo are the Palladium Pataugas boots issued to French troops in the early 1950s. (Author's collection)

next rung down on the organisational ladder were the commands of the regular and interzone forces with the latter overseeing provincial and more localised forces. Later, developments included the creation of an intelligence service, a political service, as well as different offices overseeing personnel and operations, et cetera

As a means of ensuring that the DRV's 'message' reached as many people as possible to encourage popular support and recruitment, centralised authority was decentralised through the use of a system that found its roots in the district-village administrative structure set up by the French. In areas with little or no French military presence, administration for local matters was carried out by a Village Administrative Committee (*Uy Ban Hanh Chinh Xa*) guided by cadres of the Vietnamese Communist Party. Next up in the hierarchy was the inter-village group (*lien xa*), and above this, a district committee often referred to as the Resistance Administration Committee (*Uy Ban Khang Chien Hang Chinh*), a province (*tinh*) committee, a zone (*khu*) committee and an interzone committee (*lien khu*). All the different levels of administration were responsible for generating and

mobilising support for the Viet Minh, as well as supplying volunteers and raising food for the army.

From a purely military perspective, the PAVN relied on a similar pyramidal structure of local, regional and national forces, all acting within three main defence areas determined by the CND: the Bac Bo (Tonkin); the Trung Bo (Annam); and the Nam Bo (Cochinchina). Further military division of Vietnam came through the creation of 14 zones, or *khu*, from 1945 and from March 1948, the country was split into six interzones. Most of the First Indochina War was fought in interzones 1, 2, and 3 (Tonkin).

Though the number of VM volunteers was relatively low at the time of Japan's surrender (around 5,000), the arrival of French forces boosted recruitment so that the PAVN could count on around 60,000 regular soldiers (*Chu Luc*) including around 15,000 Japanese deserters. By the end of the period dealt with in this volume (1949), VM forces totalled 250,000 (75,000 regulars, plus 175,000 regional and local forces).[28] By mid-1947, 45,000 of these troops were to be found in Tonkin, around 20,000 thousand operated in Annam and around 18,000 VM were active in Cochinchina. Much smaller

VM regulars of the 102 'Capital' Regiment in Hanoi, December 1946. (Author's collection)

VM guerrilla fighters during the Battle of Hanoi. (Author's collection)

a trip wire, making bamboo whips also released by a trip wire and placing barbed metal spikes on a wooden plank that was sent swinging down from a tree into its victim. Known as the Mace or the Tiger Trap, this deadly trap was perhaps the most feared by French (and US) troops.

As was the case in regard to political organisation, the populations of different villages could be grouped together to form larger units to carry out more significant military operations. These local militias were only raised when necessary and if required, were responsible for the small-scale sabotage of infrastructure, maintaining supply lines or even attacking small French outposts. Often, the best fighters from these inter-village units were a source of provision for the regional units (*Bo Doi Dia Phuong Quan*), each typically responsible for military actions in a given province. A regional unit usually comprised an HQ, three 135-men companies of riflemen plus a company of engineers. Their role was to carry out larger guerrilla attacks, to train the local populations in the use of weapons and to provide support for the *Bo Doi Chu Luc*, or the DRV's regular army.

Many of these regulars being trained in China from 1949, the *Chu Luc*, made up of divisions and regiments, was only used in major engagements against French forces. Forming a reserve, most French troops in Indochina (certainly before 1950) only encountered the lower echelons of the Democratic Republic of Vietnam's (DRV) armed forces. This is not to say that the VM lacked formal infantry:

numbers of VM soldiers could be found in Cambodia, Laos and at bases in Thailand.

Additionally, the VM could rely on around 20,000 militia and self-defence units (*Tu Ve*) and inter-village formations called *Dan Quan* and *Dan Quan Du Kich* units. The first was an unarmed group of women, children and those too old to fight, that could be called up to perform tasks such as working as coolies or guides. The second was a small militia group that usually contained 15 men or women guerrillas armed with rifles, grenades and other weapons used for hand-to-hand fighting. Often, the groups with an intimate knowledge of local areas, set up booby traps intended to kill or maim enemy soldiers. These traps were sometimes made from sharpened punji sticks or filled with snakes whilst other methods included placing a hand grenade in a tin can that was triggered by

France's Recruitment of Vietnamese Partisans

While most of the 9e DIC was withdrawn from Cochinchina and sent to Tonkin in February 1946, the role of continuing the pacification of Vietnam's southern regions fell to the 3e DIC. A division made up of just over 13,000 troops also known as the *Troupes Françaises de l'Indochine du Sud*, it mainly consisted of two infantry regiments, the 22e and 43e RICs who were assigned to the Bien Hoa (east of Saigon) and Can Tho (Mekong Delta) sectors. Securing the northern sectors of Cochinchina fell to the BEO, then the 13e DBLE while the areas west of Saigon (Vaico) was controlled by the 10e and 4e RACs.

Commanded by General Georges Nyo, the early months of 1946 saw the 3e DIC's operations extend southwards to Ca Mau and eastwards towards the coastal city of Nha Trang.[36] However, and in a similar fashion to the problems faced by French forces in September 1945, Nyo's efforts to seize greater control were hindered by a shortage of manpower. Effectively, the 13,000 men of the 3e DIC divided into two battalions were expected to cover 6,000 square kilometres of Vietnamese territory each. Nyo's solution, like Nguyen Binh, was to recruit up to 5,000 indigenous

Vietnamese to perform three different roles. The first was to reinforce French troops when needed (*supplétifs*); the second to act as guides, porters, cooks et cetera (*auxiliaires*); and the third to guard French outposts or integrate French commando units (*partisans des unités autochtones légères*, or *partisans de village*).

The number of partisans recruited by Nyo reached nearly 13,000 by November 1947 (thus doubling forces available),[37] so another source of local reinforcements came in the shape of the Cao Dai, a militant politico-religious sect founded in 1926. The sect venerated Buddha, Confucius, Lao Tze (the founder of Taoism[38]) and Christ but had faith in one God (Dao). By the beginning of the Second World War, it numbered nearly two million virulently anti-French members. The Cao Dai remaining nominally neutral during the Second World War, by June 1946 it had turned against the Viet Minh and around 2,000 of its partisans began to support French military efforts. Lastly, French forces in southern Vietnam were bolstered by the reformation of a gendarmerie known as the *Garde républicaine de Cochinchine* (GRC) made up of nearly 8,000 men deployed into four regiments by the end of 1947.

Table 4

Weapons known to have been used by the Viet Minh from 1946

NB. Note that some came into use after 1949. Captured from French unless specified.

Pistols	
	Nambu Type 14 (Japan: captured from Japanese)
	Colt M1911 (USA)
	Tokarev TT-33 (supplied by USSR)
	Browning/Ingliss Hi-Power (USA)
	M1935A (France)
	Model 1892 revolver (France)
Rifles (bolt-action)	
	Enfield M1917 (USA)
	Lee-Enfield (UK)
	Lebel Model 1886 (France)
	Type 99/38 rifle (Japan: captured from Japanese)
	Hanyang 88 (bought in China)
	Moisin-Nagant M1891 (supplied by USSR and China)
	MAS Modèle 36 (France)
	M1903 Springfield (probably provided by USA in 1945)
Rifle (semi-automatic)	
	M1 Carbine (USA)
Submachine guns	
	Lanchester submachine gun (UK: probably bought in Malaysia)
	Madsen M-50 (Denmark)
	Manufacture d'Arme de Toule (MAT) Modèle 49 (France)
	PPSh 41 (supplied by USSR)
	MP-40 (German)
	Thompson submachine gun (USA)
Medium machine guns	
	Pulemyot Maxima M1910 (supplied by USSR)
	Degtyaryov machine gun (supplied by USSR)
	ZB vz. 26 (Czechoslovakia: supplied by USSR)
	Browning Automatic Rifle (USA)
	Vickers .303 machine gun (UK)
Heavy machine guns	
	Hotchkiss M1929 (USA)
	Type 3 (Taisho 14) heavy machine gun (Japan: captured from Japanese)
	Type 92 machine gun (Japan: captured from Japanese)
	DShK 1938 (supplied by USSR)
Mortars	
	Brandt Modèle 1935 (France)

in January 1946, the PAVN created its first regiment, the 102 'Capital' Regiment for operations in and around Hanoi. Consisting of Regiments 36, 88, and 102, in January 1947 the 'Capital' Regiment was renamed the 308 'Vanguard' Division. By the end of 1949, the 308 was made up of three full infantry regiments, one heavy weapons regiment plus support units.[29]

The Viet Minh's Weapons

'Weapons are an important, but not decisive, factor in war. The decisive factor is the man and not the weapon'. Mao, *On Protracted War*, 1938.

As the Viet Minh lacked the usual structures and income necessary for the production of weapons, most of what it used during the early days of its war against France came from a variety of sources. For example, Giap's men captured large amounts of ammunition and rifles from the French when they overran Phai Kat on 24 December 1944 and Na Gam the following day;[30] the OSS supplied the Viet Minh with small arms and rifles from July 1945; and the Japanese turned over weapons to the Viet Minh after Japan's capitulation in August 1945. The booty obtained from the Japanese at this point included AA guns. Otherwise, the VM possessed its own armaments department headed by Tran Dai Nghia who met Ho Chi Minh during a visit to Paris in early 1946. Due to Nghia's scientific background, Ho appointed him chief of artillery of the Vietnam People's Army and in November 1946, Nghia and his colleagues began to test anti-tank guns based on the US bazooka. The first of many weapons Nghia produced for the VM, in 1949 he went on to design a recoilless rifle named the SKZ (*Sung khong giat*) and a larger recoilless artillery piece called the DKZ (*Phao khong giat*).

Other weapon-producing factories could be found across Vietnam. According to one source, several hundred former Japanese soldiers worked at Thai Nguyen and produced 50 rifles and 10 SMGs per day; 300 men and women worked under the direction of a former major in the IJA at Quang Ngai (South Central Vietnam). That former Japanese soldiers were involved in the manufacture of weapons for the VM, should come as no surprise. Indeed, while some estimates put the number of ex-IJA soldiers siding with the VM at 700,[31] other research indicates that the same soldiers provided training to the VM and even took part in some battles against the French.[32]

Similar weapons production reportedly took place at Phu To (Tonkin), at Thap Muoi (Cochinchina) – this time involving Japanese soldiers and German deserters from the French Foreign Legion – in Anna, and at Tra Ling on the border with China, Chinese technicians made rifles which were then smuggled into Tonkin.[33] By October 1950, the Viet Minh had established an arsenal in every province they controlled and a workshop in every district.[34] In the first half of 1948, the arsenal in one particular area produced 38,000 grenades, 30,000 rounds of rifle ammunition, 8,000 rounds of light machine gun ammunition, 60 rounds for rocket launchers and 100 mines. Another area produced 61

Coventry armoured car. The abysmal state of French industry in the immediate post Second World War period meant that armoured vehicles such as the Coventry had to be procured from France's allies. Available sources give the number of Coventry AVs used in Indochina at between 40 and 64. They were assigned for use by two regiments, the 1er *Régiment de Chasseurs à Cheval* (1er RCC) and the 5e *Régiment de Cuirassiers* (5e RC). When the former was transferred to operate in the Tonkin, the regiment's Coventrys were taken over by the 5e RC. (Artwork by David Bocquelet)

Humber armoured car. One source gives the number of Humbers in French service in Indochina (1946–1949) at 41. From February 1946, the Humbers – another British AV put into service by the 5e RC – were used by all three of the regiment's squadrons (plus one other 'rankless' squadron or '*escadron hors-rang*'). The number of squadrons grew to eight after the 1er RCC was sent to Tonkin in August 1946 and after the disbandment of the *Groupement Blindé du Cambodge*. (Artwork by David Bocquelet)

T30 HMC (heavy motor carriage). It is unclear how many T30 HMCs were used in Indochina and precisely, by which armoured unit. What is known is that the T30 was developed by the White Motor Company headquartered in Cleveland, Ohio in 1941. Used as a stopgap by US forces until other AVs became available (hence the reason the vehicle never received an 'M' number), the T30 resembled the White Company's own M3 half-track. One major difference was that the T30 was designed to be a howitzer vehicle and therefore, had a much higher elevation than the M3. The T30's gun was mounted behind the cab. Only 500 T30s were ever produced and soon after its introduction into US service in 1942, it was already being replaced by the M8 Scott HMC. (Artwork by David Bocquelet)

Japanese Type 89 Chi-Rho medium tank. Eleven tanks were left by the Japanese on their retreat from Phnom Penh in August 1945. Gratefully put into service by the French, the Type 89 Chi-Rho, Type 95 Ha-Gos and at least one Type 89 I-Go, were used first by the *Groupement Blindé du Cambodge* (GBC), then by the 5e RC. Tanks used by these units would, therefore, wear the emblem of the 5e RC (a Polish eagle) and the French flag. (Artwork by David Bocquelet)

Japanese Type-95 Ha-Go light tank as operated by the French forces in Tonkin during 1946-1947. (Artwork by David Bocquelet)

Landing Craft Vehicle & Personnel (LCVP) were used by each of the 10 naval assault divisions (*Dinassaut*) in Indochina after their creation in 1947. Used alongside Landing Craft Tank (LCT), Landing Craft Assault (LCA), or Landing Craft Mechanised (LCM), the LCVP operated both in Cochinchina and in Tonkin along the Mekong Delta and the Red River Delta. Notably, the LCVP was used during operations *Léa* and *Ceinture* (both in 1947). (Artwork by David Bocquelet)

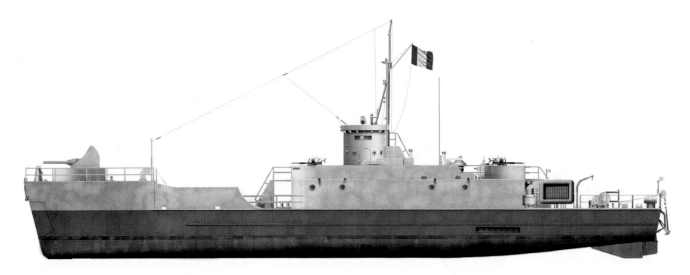

Another landing craft used by *Dinassaut* forces was the Landing Craft Infantry (LCI). This type of craft was often used to supplement the smaller LCAs and LCVPs, as a way of getting more troops ashore before a bridgehead or dock could be built or captured. The 18 LCIs used by French forces between 1946 and 1954, were designed to carry up to 200 men and were typically armed with four or five Oerlikon 20mm cannons mounted inside a round gun tub. (Artwork by David Bocquelet)

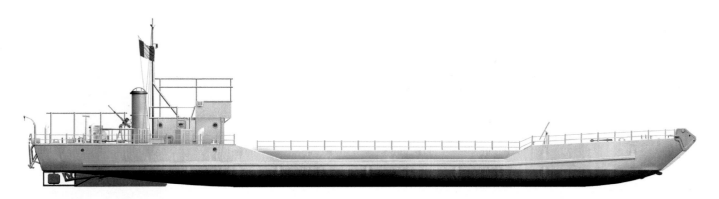

The British-built LCT Mk.4 was designed to be used in the English Channel during the Second World War. The equivalent of the American Landing Ship, Tank (LST), the LCT Mk.4 could carry and deploy up to six medium tanks or 300 tons of stores. One particular advantage for French *Dinassaut* forces using this type of craft in Indochina, was that it could operate in water as shallow as three feet. Whereas four LCTs were being used by French forces in 1946–1947, by 1954 their utility was such that riverine forces were using as many as 13 LCTs. (Artwork by David Bocquelet)

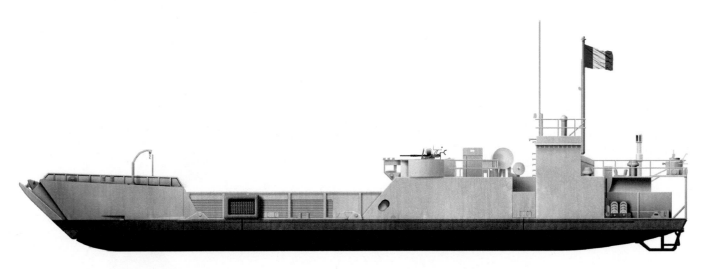

A shorter version of the LCT Mk.4, the seven LCT Mk.6s used by French forces only operated in Cochinchina due to its lack of speed (6.5 knots fully loaded) and its inability to operate in rough waters. Often used when other options were unavailable, it was also used as a floating workshop. Its armament typically consisted of two 20mm Oerlikon cannons. (Artwork by David Bocquelet)

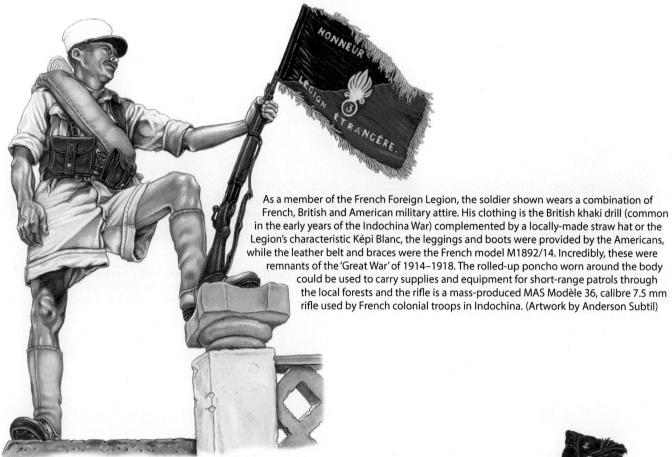

As a member of the French Foreign Legion, the soldier shown wears a combination of French, British and American military attire. His clothing is the British khaki drill (common in the early years of the Indochina War) complemented by a locally-made straw hat or the Legion's characteristic Képi Blanc, the leggings and boots were provided by the Americans, while the leather belt and braces were the French model M1892/14. Incredibly, these were remnants of the 'Great War' of 1914–1918. The rolled-up poncho worn around the body could be used to carry supplies and equipment for short-range patrols through the local forests and the rifle is a mass-produced MAS Modèle 36, calibre 7.5 mm rifle used by French colonial troops in Indochina. (Artwork by Anderson Subtil)

Making their first appearance at the end of Second World War the Female Auxiliaries of the French Armed Forces were active participants in all of France's post-war colonial conflicts. This Second Lieutenant (sous-lieutenant) was a nurse or doctor in the Marine Brigade from the Far East but many other women served in Indochina in various roles. These ranged from secretaries to mechanics and later, as aeromedical rescue helicopter pilots. Here, is shown the light green uniform worn in tropical climates, lightweight suede shoes with soft soles and a brown leather handbag issued to female personnel. The uniform is topped by a black and red calot bonnet with the golden anchor of the French Navy. (Artwork by Anderson Subtil)

This is shows a Royal Artillery staff sergeant serving with the British/Indian forces that arrived in Saigon in September 1945. He was likely an assistant within the staff of Major General Sir Douglas Gracey or one of his senior officers and is shown wearing the jungle green bush shirt of the new uniform for tropical regions manufactured in India and adopted by the Indian Army from mid-1944 onwards. His rank is represented by three stripes and a single diamond in white fabric (representing the crown), sewn directly onto the right sleeve, although it was more common to use the insignia on both sleeves. The canvas belt with brass buckle pin was a design that had recently been adopted by British forces in the Far East. The same is true of the jungle green beret which is adorned with the metal badge of the Royal Artillery. (Artwork by Anderson Subtil)

This 2nd Lieutenant of the Imperial Japanese Army is shown wearing the uniform of Japanese occupying forces in Saigon towards the end of the Second World War. Wearing battle fatigue, the uniform consists of a light shirt with wide sleeves, dark green officer trousers and long brown leather boots. His rank is indicated above the right chest pocket and his characteristic field cap has extended flaps for protection from the sun. The soldier wears two belts; one is thinner than the other and is used for carrying a Nambu Type 14 pistol, while the other is adapted for a Shin Guntô Type 98 sabre. This was a mass-produced version of the *katana* used by samurai warriors. (Artwork by Anderson Subtil)

Throughout the First Indochina War, French forces procured large quantities of clothing, weapons and other equipment from its allies, something seen reflected in the attire worn by this Chasseur Parachutiste of the 1er RCP. He wears a 'Duck Hunter' camo fabric jacket issued to US Marines with French M1947 uniform pants and US Army buckle boots. Steel M1 helmets were common, but many preferred locally made fabric hats made from materials supplied by their allies. His combat equipment is a mixture of M36 braces and M23 cartridge belts which are both remnants of the Second World War. His backpack is a British 1937 model and his weaponry consists of an M8/M3 trench knife and a CR39 rifle especially adapted for use by airborne troops. (Artwork by Anderson Subtil)

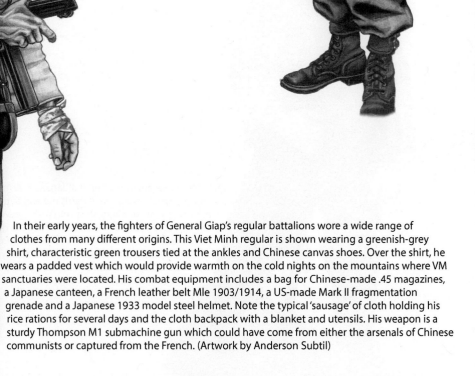

In their early years, the fighters of General Giap's regular battalions wore a wide range of clothes from many different origins. This Viet Minh regular is shown wearing a greenish-grey shirt, characteristic green trousers tied at the ankles and Chinese canvas shoes. Over the shirt, he wears a padded vest which would provide warmth on the cold nights on the mountains where VM sanctuaries were located. His combat equipment includes a bag for Chinese-made .45 magazines, a Japanese canteen, a French leather belt Mle 1903/1914, a US-made Mark II fragmentation grenade and a Japanese 1933 model steel helmet. Note the typical 'sausage' of cloth holding his rice rations for several days and the cloth backpack with a blanket and utensils. His weapon is a sturdy Thompson M1 submachine gun which could have come from either the arsenals of Chinese communists or captured from the French. (Artwork by Anderson Subtil)

Disbanded in early 1944, but re-established in late 1947, the 3rd *Régiment de Tirailleurs Marocains* (3e RTM) was sent to the Far East in March 1949, where it remained until the end of the conflict. This Moroccan '*Goumier*' of the 3e RTM is a veteran of the battles fought on the Italian front during World War II (as evidenced by the medals and decorations on the left side of his chest) and is shown wearing the traditional djellaba over the M1947 uniform. This is in addition to the characteristic Moroccan turban. The leather strap on his right shoulder carries a .9mm Parabellum calibre MAT-49 submachine gun, a weapon introduced in 1949 to complement the old MAS.38. (Artwork by Anderson Subtil)

A fact that is frequently overlooked is that around 60,000 combatants of the CEFEO forces in Indochina – 20 percent of the entire contingent – came from France's African colonies such as Senegal. The soldier of the *Régiment de Marche de Tirailleurs Sénégalais* is shown wearing the American HBT uniform and the characteristic Vietnamese fabric hat that was popular until the end of the conflict. The canvas belt and braces, canteen, ammunition pouches and backpack, were the US Army's M1936 model, while weapons included the M1A1 carbine (with a side-folding stock), an M3 dagger in its M8 Bakelite scabbard and a French M1937 grenade. (Artwork by Anderson Subtil)

The Potez 542 was a derivative of the Potez 540, powered by Lorraine 12Hfrs Pétrel V-12 engines, with 720hps. A total of 74 were built, with some exported to Spain. By September 1939, nearly all were transferred to the French colonies in North Africa and Indochina, where they continued serving for transport purposes and paratrooper service. Having poor defensive armament and proving vulnerable to modern fighters, they were all withdrawn from service by late 1943. (Artwork by Jean-Marie Guillou)

The Loire 130 was a 'flying boat' made by Loire Aviation of St. Nazaire in the 1930s, in response to the requirement from the French Navy for a reconnaissance aircraft that could serve aboard battleships and cruisers. It entered series production in 1937 and except on battleships and cruisers, served aboard the seaplane tender Commandant Teste. Although proving obsolete and having only marginal performance, it remained in service throughout the Second World War. This example was operated by the squadron 8S in Indochina of the 1940s and saw operations during the war against Thailand in 1941. (Artwork by Jean-Marie Guillou)

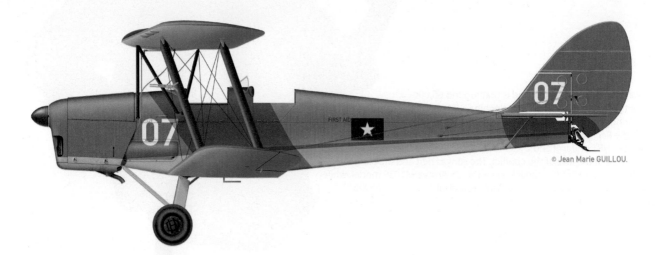

One of two aircraft donated to the Peoples' Army of Vietnam (PAVN) by Bao Dai in 1945 (the other was a MS.500), this Tiger Moth became one of the first aircraft used by the Vietnamese Air Force on its establishment in August 1949. At the controls was Nguyen Due Viet. On its first flight, the aircraft was damaged and remained out of service until July 1954. (Artwork by Jean-Marie Guillou)

The Mitsubishi G4M 'Betty' was IJNAF's most renowned torpedo-bomber. This twin-engined aircraft was responsible for sinking HMS *Prince of Wales* and HMS *Repulse* on 10 December 1941. This example of the 13th Koku Kantai Yuso-tai was amongst a total of about 64 IJAAF and IJNAF aircraft collected by the ATAIU-SEA, and prepared for shipment to the UK for flight-testing. Due to the lack of shipping space, only four actually reached Great Britain: a number were donated to the French once the ATAIU-SEA was disbanded at Seletar AB in Singapore on 15 May 1946. AdA flew them as transports. (Artwork by Jean-Marie Guillou)

The ATAIU-SEA obtained an unknown number of Mitsubishi A6M 'Zero' fighters. Most were A6M2s of the 381st Kokutai, captured in Malaya. They were of particular interest for their ability to outmanoeuvre virtually any fighter in Allied service and were flight-tested at Tebrau AB through late 1945 and early 1946. Following the disbandment of the ATAIU, they served as the back bone of the so-called Gremlin Task Force, before an unknown number – at least one – perhaps up to three – ended up in the French service. (Artwork by Jean-Marie Guillou)

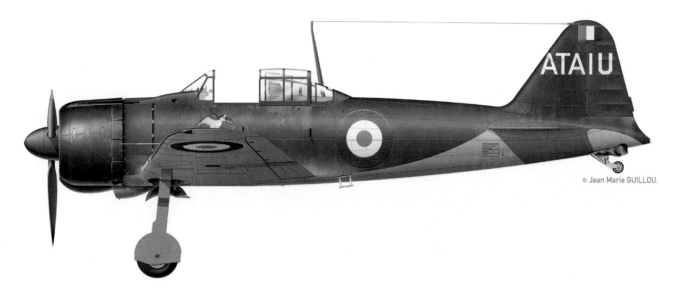

This is a reconstruction of the only Zero confirmed as test-flown by the French, who proved impressed by the type. It remains unclear if the aircraft was over painted in dark green overall, as many of airframes test-flown by the ATAIU-SEA were, but it seems that its under surfaces were left in caramel colour. French national insignia was applied instead of the Royal Air Force and the French flag applied atop of the fin, above the ATAIU title in white. (Artwork by Jean-Marie Guillou)

The Kokusai Ki-86 was based on the Swedish-designed Bücker Bü.131 Jungmann and used primarily as a trainer aircraft, with a secondary capability to be armed as a light bomber. The ATAIU quickly learned to appreciate the Japanese capability to modify (and better) the European models and retained up to a dozen for training purposes. All were painted in dark green on top surfaces and sides and received the suitable insignia. Notably, the French did not follow in fashion and never operated the Ki-86. (Artwork by Jean-Marie Guillou)

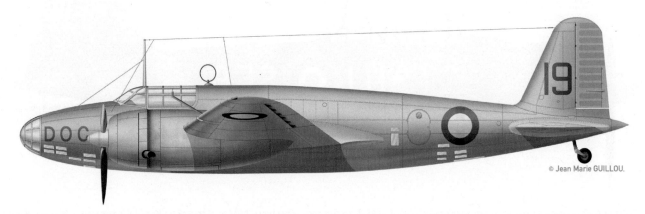

Also known as the Type 97 Heavy Bomber, the Mitsubishi Ki-21 IIB 'Sally' was used by the IJAAF for long-range bombing missions. The Gremlin Task Force adopted at least four Sallies: No. 14 (which wore no name), No. 10 ('F/Lt Lyne Chute'), No. 19 (nick-named 'Doc', shown here) and No. 17 ('Happy'). There is some uncertainty whether they were painted in white or in (strongly bleached) caramel colour overall or on upper surfaces and sides only (if the latter then they might have had their undersurfaces in 'bare metal'). However, it is certain they wore blue and white South East Asia Command roundels instead of their original Hinomarus. All had their armament removed. The GT I/34 of the *Armée de l'Air* also briefly used a single 'Sally': this was operated from February 1946, but destroyed in a crash already two months later. (Artwork by Jean-Marie Guillou)

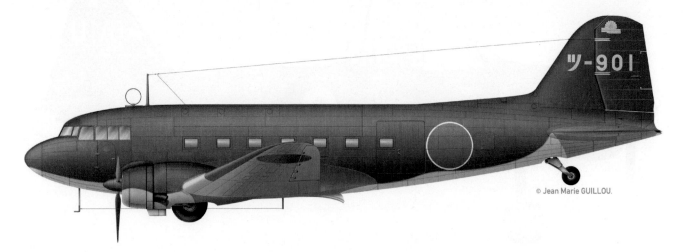

From a numerical point of view, the Showa/Nakajima L2D3 'Tabby' – a licence-built version of the Douglas DC-3 – was the most important Japanese transport aircraft used in the Second World War. This example also survived long enough to be deployed by the French *Section avions de liaison* (SAL). (Artwork by Jean-Marie Guillou)

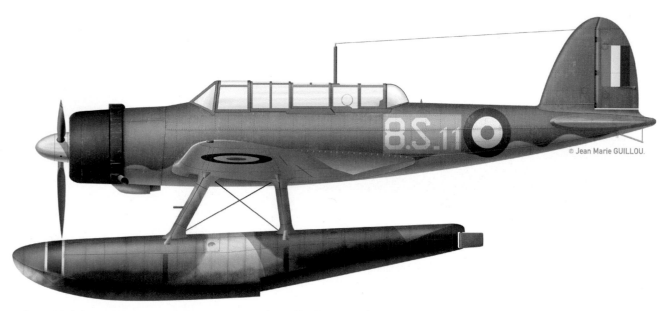

The Aichi E13A 'Jake' was a long-range reconnaissance aircraft used by the IJNm, which could carry crew of three and a bombload of 250kg (550lbs). Over a dozen were captured from the Japanese: one was operated by the Royal New Zealand Air Force for liaison purposes, while four out of other seven found in working condition, were pressed into service by the squadron 8S of the French Naval Aviation. While some were painted in medium grey overall, this example originally retained the dark green livery on upper surfaces and sides. (Artwork by Jean-Marie Guillou)

The Nakajima Ki-43 Hayabusa ('Oscar', formally 'Army Type 1 Fighter') was a single-seater tactical fighter first used by the IJAAF since October 1941. Together with the Zero, it belonged to the last generation of light, easy to fly, highly manoeuvrable (but also lightly armed) combat aircraft. They proved highly popular in service for their pleasant flight characteristics and excellent manoeuvrability. Unsurprisingly, after Japan's capitulation, numerous examples were adapted for service with the Gremlin Force at first. (Artwork by Jean-Marie Guillou)

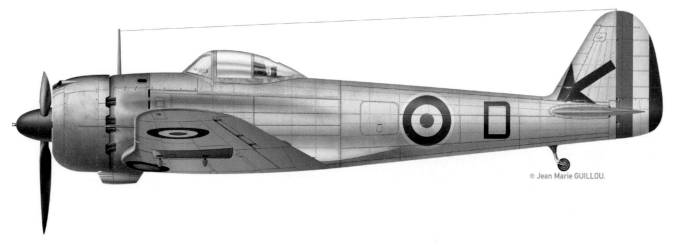

By February 1946, as additional Ki-43s were recovered and repaired, no less than 30 were in service with the *Armée de l'Air's* GC I/17 and II/17, both of which were based at Tan Son Nhut Air Base, outside Saigon. By this time, the dark green colour was usually completely removed, though many received underwing hardpoints for bombs calibre 30kg. (Artwork by Jean-Marie Guillou)

As of the end of February 1946, GC II/7 and the SAL were operating four Mitsubishi Ki-46 Dinah twin-engine aircraft (Army Type 100 Command Reconnaissance Aircraft). The Armée de l'Air initially flew them for evaluation purposes, but continued flying them for liaison and reconnaissance until mid-1946, when they were replaced by DC-3s. (Artwork by Jean-Marie Guillou)

The first of French-manufactured transport aircraft of the *Armée de l'Air* to reach Indochina after the Japanese capitulation, were Junkers Ju-52 captured after the collapse of Nazi Germany. In November 1945, 18 Ju-52s of the CT 1/34 were deployed to Bien Hoa, Nha Trang and Tan Son Nhut, where the unit operated them together with several Japanese types, before being integrated into the GT I/64. The later brought to Indochina the French-manufactured AAC.1 Toucans and was followed by the Bach Mai-deployed GT II/64, which arrived in July 1947, one of whose aircraft is shown here. (Artwork by Jean-Marie Guillou)

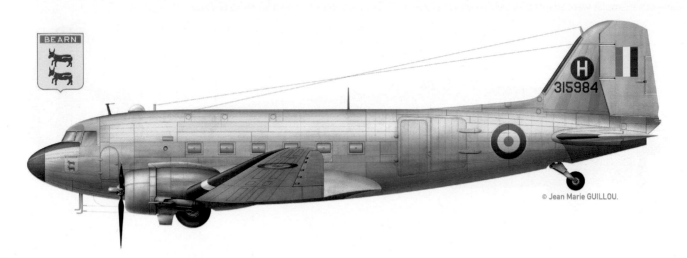

The Douglas C-47 Skytrain or Dakota (RAF designation) was developed from the civilian Douglas DC-3 airliner and deployed extensively during the Second World War. Complementing its AAC.1 Toucans, the *Armée de l'Air* began deploying them in large numbers in Indochina starting in mid-1946. This example – left in bare metal overall – was operated by the GT I/64, as seen during the Operation Léa, in October 1947. The type was deployed both for transport and as a bomber. (Artwork by Jean-Marie Guillou)

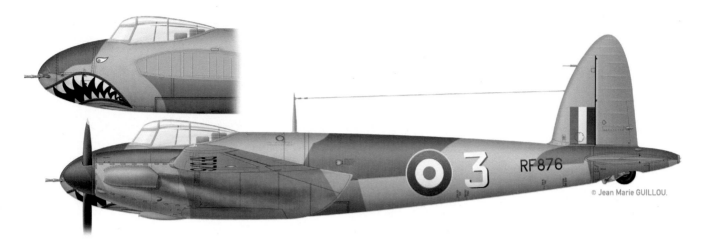

As the crisis in the Indochina continued to grow, in January 1947 the *Armée de l'Air* re-deployed the GC I/3 to Tan Son Nhut AB. The unit was equipped with de Havilland Mosquito VI and XVI fighter-bombers and starting in March 1947, deployed in support of operations to secure the areas west of Saigon. One disadvantage of the aircraft was that its wooden frame was ill-adapted to the humid conditions present in Indochina. (Artwork by Jean-Marie Guillou)

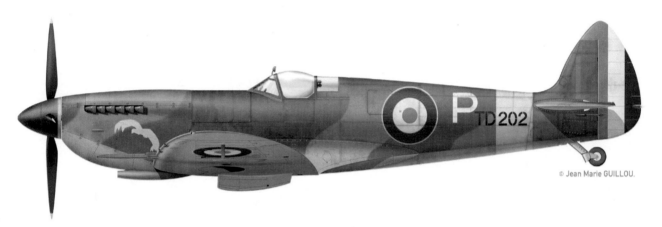

30 Supermarine Spitfire LF.Mk. IXs were supplied by Great Britain in late 1945 and first used by the AdA around the Plain of Reeds, as French forces began to hunt down the Viet Minh. The example with the serial number TD202 was a LF.Mk IX equipped with Merlin 66 engine of 1580hp, optimised for low-altitude operations. It was originally manufactured to the 17th Contract for Spitfires, passed in April 1944 and including 5,663 aircraft, mostly constructed b Vickers Armstrong. Originally, it was equipped with a camera port on the left side of the fuselage, behind the cockpit, but this was removed by the time it entered service with the GC II/7, in 1946. (Artwork by Jean-Marie Guillou)

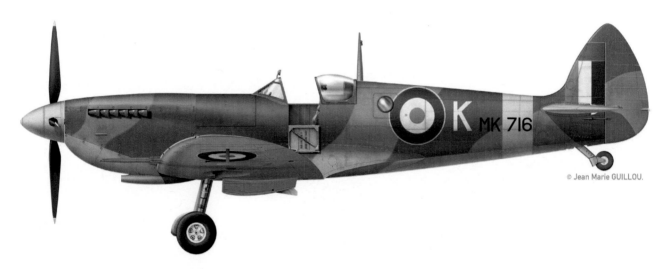

The French-operated Spitfire LF.Mk IXs retained their original camouflage pattern in dark green and dark grey over with medium grey undersides, and the fuselage band in sky colour. Contrary to the TD202 shown above, this example – serial MK716 – belonged to the 5th Spitfire contract, ordered in 1940 and originally made as an F.Mk IX, equipped with the Merlin 61 engine. By the time, it was handed over to the GC II/7, it was upgraded to LF.Mk IX standard, but retained its fin-tips and the camera-port behind the cockpit. French Spitfires were gradually phased out from 1949 and replaced by Grumman F8F Bearcats. (Artwork by Jean-Marie Guillou)

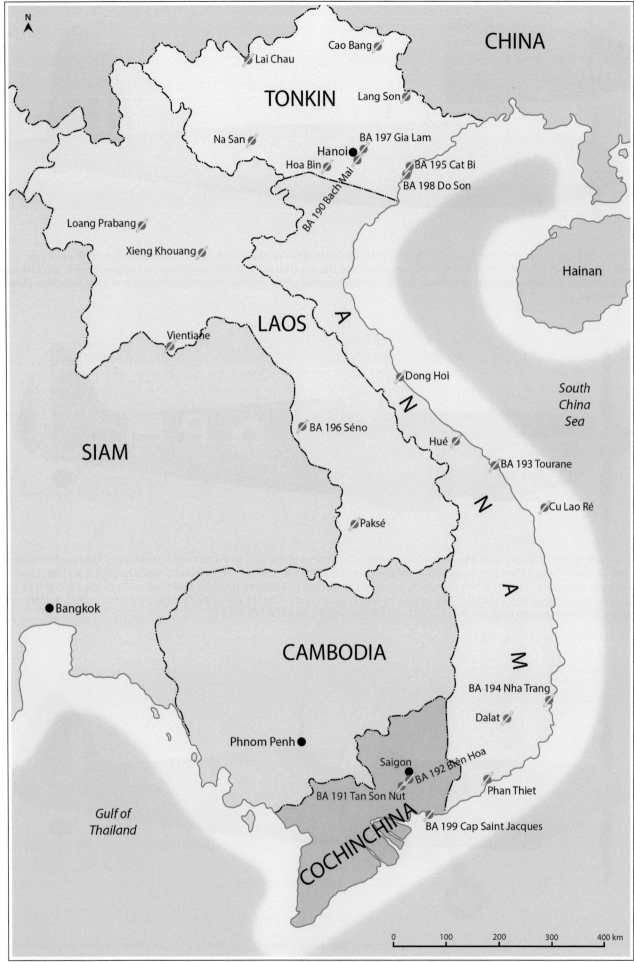

N

CHINA

Cao Bang

Lai Chau

TONKIN

Lang Son

Na San

BA 197 Gia Lam

Hanoi

Hoa Bin

BA 195 Cat Bi

BA 198 Do Son

BA 190 Bach Mai

Loang Prabang

Xieng Khouang

Hainan

LAOS

Vientiane

Dong Hoi

South
China
Sea

SIAM

BA 196 Séno

Hué

BA 193 Tourane

Cu Lao Ré

Paksé

Bangkok

CAMBODIA

BA 194 Nha Trang

Dalat

Phnom Penh

Saigon

BA 192 Bien Hoa

BA 191 Tan Son Nut

Phan Thiet

Gulf of
Thailand

BA 199 Cap Saint Jacques

COCHINCHINA

0   100   200   300   400 km

A map of the French Indochina with major airfields and air bases of the late 1940s. (Map by George Anderson)

	Lance Grenades (grenade launcher) 50mm M1937 (France)	
	M1 mortar (USA)	
	M2 4.2-inch mortar (USA)	
Anti-tank weapons		
	M3 37mm anti-tank gun (USA)	
	Ordnance QF (quick-firing) 6-pdr (UK)	
	PIAT (projector, infantry, anti-tank) (UK)	
	Type 94 37mm anti-tank gun (Japan: captured from Japanese)	
	60, 122, and 185mm rocket launchers (produced by VM)	
	SSAT 53 (produced by VM)	
Anti-aircraft weapons		
	Bofors 40mm (Sweden)	
	Hotchkiss M1929 (France)	
	Oerlikon 20mm cannon (France)	
	Schneider M1913, M1915, and M1917 (France)	
	Type 98 20mm AA cannon (Japan: captured from Japanese)	
Artillery		
	M1897 75mm field gun (France)	
	Ordnance QF 3.7-inch mountain howitzer (UK)	
	Schneider M1906 65mm mountain cannon (France)	
	Schneider L M1936 field cannon (France)	
	Type 38 75mm field cannon (Japan: captured from Japanese)	
	Type 92 light howitzer battalion cannon (Japan: captured from Japanese)	

Unit Profile: The 1e *Régiment Etranger de Cavalerie*

Created in 1922, in January 1947, the 1e REC arrived at Tourane from Morocco where it had boarded the *Pasteur*. Immediately deployed as infantry in the retaking of Hué from the Viet Minh in February, but also operating in central Annam, south Annam and Cochinchina, until April 1947, the unit used a variety of British armoured fighting vehicles such as the AFVW19 Coventry, Humbers, or the Carden-Loyd Universal Carrier (also known as the Bren Gun Carrier, or Bren Carrier).

Split into six squadrons, the 1st and 2nd Squadrons of the 1e REC were based in Saigon and Annam; the 3rd in Tourane; the 4th in Hué, the 5th in Dong Hoi; and the 6th at Phan Thiet, an extension of Cam Ranh Bay some 125 miles south of Saigon. In December 1947, the six squadrons were reorganised into two groups: the 1e *Groupe d'Escadrons* comprising the 1e and 2e squadrons was based at My Tho (Mekong Delta), while the other four squadrons making up the 2e *Groupe* remained as they were geographically. The squadron HQ and a maintenance squadron (*Escadron Hors Rang*) was based in Tourane.[40]

From April 1947, the unit became an amphibious unit operating in and around the 2,500 square-mile wetlands of the Plain of Reeds and the innumerable rivers and streams that cover much of Annam and Cochinchina. As seen previously, the Plain of Reeds served as a base and refuge for the Viet Minh's southern fighters.

light machine guns, 4 submachine guns, 20 semi-automatic pistols and 7,000 rounds of ammunition.[35]

The Battle of Hanoi, December 1946 and its aftermath

As the fundaments of phase 1 of the *dau tranh* strategy were consolidated around the Viet Minh's strongholds in Tonkin, tensions caused by France's seizing unilateral control of Haiphong, then Lang Son, in November 1946 were compounded as French troops were landed at Tourane that same month. This was in violation of the 6 March Accords and an action that convinced the DRV that France was planning to invade Tonkin. The first weeks of December saw a complete breakdown of relations between Vietnamese and French officials. The result being that on 19 December 1946, the Viet Minh smuggled explosives past French Army guards and destroyed the city's power supply. With Hanoi plunged into darkness, more Viet Minh began to attack French positions thus starting the Battle of Hanoi and the First Indochina War.

Though Giap's forces had hoped for a quick victory, General Molière had deployed French forces in such a way to ensure that different sectors of Hanoi were well protected by around 4,500 of the 1e and 3e RICs, the GBT, a battalion of paratroopers, and an artillery platoon manning two batteries of 105mm guns.[39] The sheer power of the French deployment meant that the daily ongoings of life in Hanoi were restored within four days and from 23 December

1946, Molière's attention then turned to preventing further attacks and clearing areas of potential threats from the Viet Minh.

As the hunt continued up to mid-February 1947, Giap's forces in the south simply retreated to the forests, valleys and mountains of Cochinchina to await further orders and to avoid the type of mass face-to-face conventional confrontation that the French so desperately wanted and the type of war for which they had prepared.

In the apparent absence of this form of confrontation, Nyo pushed forward with setting up a system whereby Cochinchina was split into three 'pacification zones' that roughly corresponded to the Viet Minh's war zones VII, VIII and IX. Each zone (West, East, Centre) was commanded by a colonel and the overall responsibility of the zonal system was handled by a five-man 'pacification committee'. Once the zones were in place, a further division would take place and zones were split into smaller areas. Known in French military parlance as the '*quadrillage*' (gridding) of a given area, the next phase called for a gradual 'raking', or '*ratissage*' of that area in order to eliminate any Viet Minh presence.

If this system worked to good effect in Algeria, a war that started almost immediately after Indochina, French forces in south-east Asia were never sufficient enough in number to make gridding and raking successful. To compound the troop situation even further, from 29 March 1947 to February 1949, large numbers of French forces (18,000 in 1947, 30,000 in 1948) were committed to quelling

Vehicle Profile: M29C Weasel (designated *Crabe* in French service)

The M29C Weasel was a Second World War tracked vehicle built by US-manufacturer Studebaker. Acquired by the 1er REC in late 1947, the Water Weasel version was capable of operating in inland waterways due to fore and aft float tanks and twin rudders added to the standard, semi-amphibious version. Carrying a crew of four, the Weasel was constructed using galvanised steel to form a watertight shell with a boat-like hull and steel side skirts. This design enabled the vehicle to travel through water more quickly. Inside, the vehicle was fitted with drain plugs that allowed the crew to evacuate any water that managed to penetrate the outer

shell. To steer the Weasel, a capstan directing the two rear rudders was to be found at the fore.

At just over 10ft in length and just over 5ft wide, the Weasel was powered by a Model 6-170 Champion six-cylinder and petrol-fuelled Studebaker 75 hp engine capable of reaching 36 mph on land and 3 to 20 mph in swamp areas or rice paddies. Its operational range was some 165 miles (265km) on land butas the Weasel used much more fuel when used on water, this range was reduced to 50 miles (80km). As for its weaponry, though none came as standard, a .30 calibre Bren machine gun or FM 24/29 light machine gun could be mounted midship.

From April 1947, cavalry units of the Foreign Legion exchanged armoured vehicles for those more suited to operations in Vietnam's vast network of waterways. This photo illustrates the abilities of the M29C 'Crabe' to negotiate areas in which the Viet Minh took refuge and in which they were hunted down. (Author's collection)

Another feature of the amphibious vehicle was the addition of the crab insignia pictured. Also note that the crew is wearing the US M1 helmet indicating that the photo was taken post-1950. (Author's collection)

A .30 calibre Bren or FM 24/29 LMG could be mounted midship. The photo it shows all of the four-man crew was armed. Note the canvas topping aft. (Author's collection)

The bow of this M29C clearly shows its boat-like shape. This enabled the vehicle to negotiate the rice paddies and waterways in which it operated. However, frequent stops would be made to unclog the vehicle's tracks of long grass that hampered movement. Note the LCT in the background. LCT's could transport up to 25 M29Cs at a time. (Author's collection)

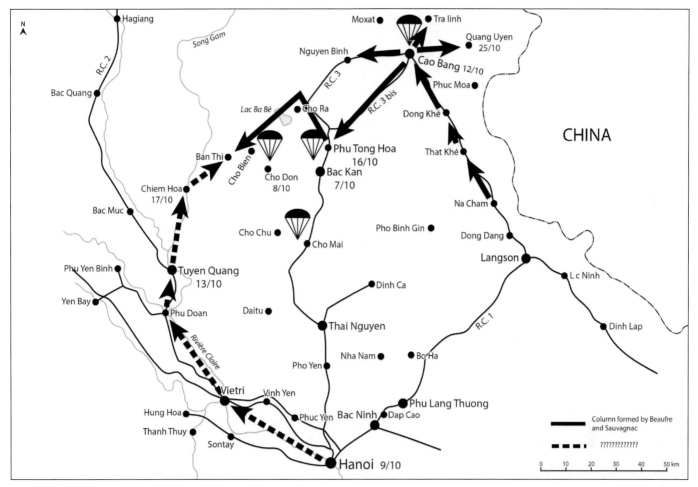

The objectives of Operation Léa were to encircle the VM's operational base and to cut off its supply routes with China. (Map by George Anderson)

large-scale civil unrest in Madagascar, another of France's colonies. Again, in contrast to the Algerian War, there was, moreover, little public interest in (or support for) a conflict taking place on the other side of the world.

As noted previously, the French population was more concerned with reconstructing a society ripped apart by five years of Nazism, a concern that prompted Socialist Premier Paul Ramadier to dispatch French writer and scholar, Paul Mus, to Indochina in a last-ditch attempt to persuade Ho Chi Minh to lay down arms and not to go to war. The latter rejected a plan for peace drawn up by Valluy and carried by Mus – he saw surrender as a form of cowardice.

Valluy's Winter Offensive, 1947

As pacification operations continued in Cochinchina, from March 1947 the attention of French commanders switched to paving the way for a large-scale attack on the Viet Minh's heartlands in Tonkin. In preparation, from February 1947, the main objectives were to secure the main road and river arteries that provided access to these areas while cutting off the Viet Minh's various supply lines, including those leading from Loas into Vietnam. Among these operations, Operation *Dédale* (January) reinforced French positions in Nam Dinh; Operation *Louis* (17 February) targeted taking control of Nui Déo on what is now the *Quoc lo 18* national road that links Ha Long and Hanoi; Operation *Catherine* (18 March) took place further up the road at Dong Trieu; Operation *Djebel* (March) and Operation *Escale II* (6–31 March) saw the French target Nam Dinh on the Thai Binh River therefore restricting maritime access to Hanoi. *Operation Georges* of March 1947 also targeted French control of the main routes between Haiphong and Hanoi, while Operation

Camille (23 March–23 April) saw efforts move westwards towards the Vietnamese border with Laos.

The objective of *Camille* was twofold: by targeting Moc Chau on the Quoc lo 43 national road, the French were able to control both the direct road access to Laos and the main link between Hanoi and Dien Bien Phu, the now Asian Highway 13. Similar objectives were reached by Operation *Papillon* (15 April–15 May) which targeted Hao Binh just east of the Rivière Noire (Black River), a tributary of one of one of Vietnam's main waterways, the Red River. Hoa Binh was also situated on one of the largest thoroughfares in western Vietnam and Laos (formerly *Route Colonial 6*).

May 1947 saw Operation *Aphrodite* that centred on the forested areas around Phu To; *Operation Marché 17* (2 May) carried out on the Plain of Reeds, while Operation *Niagara* (6–15 May) centred on areas around the Red River. By the end of July, the commander of the *Troupes Françaises de l'Indochine Nord* (TIFN), General Salan, was ready to set in motion an ambitious plan to destroy Viet Minh resistance to France once and for all. Borrowing the name of a ridge on the *Route Coloniale 3* (RC3) between Cho Ra and Phu Tong Hoa, on 26 July 1947, he authorised preparations for Operation *Léa*.

The plan Salan had in mind was to encircle the Viet Minh's main base of operations at Bac Kan and cut off supply routes from China by using three different groups totalling around 13,200 troops in 17 battalions. The first, Group 'S', was commanded by Lieutenant-Colonel Henri Sauvagnac (hence the 'S') and consisted of a detachment from the Provisional Airborne Half-Brigade (*Demi-Brigade de Marche Parachutiste*: DBMP). This force made up of 1,137 men of the 1/1er RCP, the 3/1 RCP and the 1e BPC (1e *Bataillon*

Preparations for the attack on Bac Kan in October 1947 included securing the road between Lang Son and Cao Bang. Here, French troops are shown taking a well-needed rest. (Author's collection)

Parachutiste de Choc) from France's 25e *Division Aéroportée*, was to be dropped in the Bac Kan-Cho Don-Cho Moi zone.

A second force known as Group 'B' and commanded by Colonel André Beaufre, was made up of three armoured, three infantry and three artillery battalions supported by engineering and transport battalions.[41] The role of this group of 8,000 men – some from the Moroccans of the RICM, was to advance eastwards along *Route Colonial 4* (RC4) where it was to secure the road between Lang Son and Cao Bang. From here, it would join groups 'S' and 'B' in Bac Kan.

As for Group 'C' led by Colonel Communal, this was a three-battalion, waterborne force of 4,000 men that was to make its way up the Red and Clear Rivers aboard LCTs. Long-range reconnaissance missions had been carried out by French Navy Curtiss PBY5A Catalinas while ground support was provided by Spitfire 9s of the 4th Fighter Group (EC.IV and EC.IX). As for the transportation of the DBMP, this was carried out by a 12-strong detachment flying Junkers JU-52s and AAC.1 Toucans (French-made Ju-52s) from Transport Group 1/64 'Béarn' temporarily based at Bach Mai.[42]

On the first two days of the attack (7–8 October), detachment 'A' (1e *Batallion de Parachutistes Coloniaux*) landed directly over its target areas with such precision and surprise, that it found

Paratroopers of the 1/1 RCP board a Toucan of the aviation group I/64 'Béarn' based at Bach Mai. (Author's collection)

correspondence awaiting Ho Chi Minh's signature, one of his ministers sat at his desk and Japanese and Nazi German instructors ready to give training to VM guerrillas. The latter, choosing this option rather than being tried as war criminals by Allied forces in 1945, group 'A' also managed to free around 200 French and Vietnamese hostages captured by the VM in Hanoi in December 1946 and captured the main radio transmitter for the 'Voice of Vietnam', one of

The drop over Bac Kan, 7 October 1947. While the French attacked this settlement in central Tonkin, another operation, *Lison*, was simultaneously taking place in the High Region between the Black and Red rivers. The objective of *Lison* was to secure the road (now the CT05) between Nghia lo and Lao Cai on the northern border with China, one of the VM's main supply routes. (Author's collection)

Clearing up operations continued once Bac Kan had been taken back from VM control. Here, French troops negotiate some of the challenging terrain of Tonkin. (Author's collection)

A Soldier of the First Indochinese War: Emile Olivier (1921–1959)

Emile Olivier was born in Saint-Amand-les-Eaux in northern France on 21 August 1921. First a member the French Resistance in the Calais region, in early 1944 Olivier joined the 1st French Army and took part in fighting to liberate the north-eastern French city of Colmar from its occupation by Nazi German troops. Promoted to second lieutenant on 1 June 1945, he was then transferred to the 10th Company of the 6th Regiment of Colonial Infantry (10/6e RIC). Leaving France and arriving in Saigon as part of the CEFEO on 16 November 1945, Olivier then took part in operations to secure Nam Dinh. On 23–24 December, his platoon was attacked by 300

Captain Emile Oliver. (Author's collection)

VM, led by Japanese soldiers resulting in the loss of a third of the platoon's men.

Promoted to Lieutenant in July 1947, Olivier took part in Operation *Lison* from 7–14 October of that year. After returning to France in February 1948, Olivier was transferred to the training centre of the 1e *Brigade de Commandos Coloniaux* (1e BCC) in March 1949. Obtaining his parachutist wings in May 1949, he returned to Indochina in December and was to join the 8th then the 3rd Battalion of the BCC. His service in the 3e BCC saw Olivier sent to Laos in September 1950 and in mid-October, he took part

in fighting around RC4 and That Khé. Olivier was taken prisoner by the VM on 20 October 1950 and on 16 January 1951, he made his first attempt at escape. Recaptured after 10 days in the jungle around Lang Son, Olivier was interned at Cao Bang then That Khé. A second attempt at escape in March 1951 was successful and 12 days later he reached a French outpost at Pho Cu. After then serving with South Vietnamese and Laotian troops, Olivier returned to France in June 1952 where he was promoted to the rank of captain that October.

Olivier returned to Indochina in 1954 to serve with the 1e BCC before being sent to Algeria in October 1955. Olivier's service in the Algerian War saw him take part in battles around Marabout de Djedida, at the Oued Hallail and at Port Said in Egypt during Suez Crisis. He was then to become second in command to Roger Trinquier (one of France's most renowned counterinsurgency theorists) before becoming an instructor at the training centre of the BCC in Bayonne in April 1957. A second tour of service in Algeria resulted in Olivier's death on 6 November 1959. For his service in the Second World War, Indochina and Algeria, Olivier was decorated 13 times and mentioned in dispatches on nine occasions. Posthumously awarded the French Legion of Honour.

the Viet Minh's most effective tools of propaganda. Over 260 VM were killed in the attacks.

Meanwhile, group 'B' had left Lang Son and had made its way eastwards along *Route Coloniale* 4 (RC4) where it was to secure the road to Cao Bang and cut off the VM's escape and supply route with China. Joined by more paratroopers, after three days fighting

its way through Phu Thong Hua, 'B' joined 'S' at Bac Kan on 16 October. Group 'C' had started its move northwards on 9 October, then encountered sandbanks along the way and was forced to land a contingent of its force at Tuyên Quang. The remainder of the force was now stranded in enemy territory, its LCTs were freed from their clogged-up positions by engineers of 'B' who had made their way southwards.[43]

While the objectives of the first phase of Operation *Léa* were now accomplished, a second phase consisted of raking the forested areas surrounding the targeted cities and these clearing operations continued until the 8 November 1947, a full month after the first phase had begun. French forces also managed to capture or destroy many of the Viet Minh's weapons factories situated in the middle region of Tonkin, whilst similar objectives were reached in the higher regions of Tonkin through Operation *Lison* between 7–14 October. The operation targeting the areas between Nghia lo and Lao Cai on the border with China was another month-long operation – this time codenamed *Ceinture* (belt) and began on 20 November.

Here, 18 battalions, 18 LCs and paratroopers were given the mission of encountering and defeating VM regular units of the VM's 'Capital Regiment' and its elite force, the 'Doc Lap', stationed in and around an area to the north and northwest of Hanoi. Yet again, the VM proved to be masters at escaping enemy forces and the guerrillas simply dissolved back into the Vietnamese landscape

to fight another day and wait for the right moment to launch its own deadly offensive. Another seven years would pass until that day came. In the meantime, 1947 proved to be the year when France suffered its highest casualties. Throughout that year, 5,345 of its soldiers were killed and another 9,790 were injured.

The My Trach Massacre

As one of the least known events of the First Indochina War, the My Trach Massacre of 29 November 1947, bears a striking resemblance to the My Lai Massacre that occurred in March 1968 at the hands of US troops. The My Trach Massacre took place in My Trach village, My Thuy commune, Le Thuy District in the Quang Binh province from five to eight o'clock. During the operation, French soldiers burnt 326 houses and killed more than half of the villagers of My Trach. Many women were raped before being killed and of the 300 killed, 170 were women and 157 children. The event is commemorated at the 'Day of Hatred' in Vietnam.

4
MEANWHILE, IN LAOS AND CAMBODIA

It is natural that this volume should devote most of its pages to this aspect of the conflict given that most of the fighting of the First Indochina War took place in Tonkin. However, to complete our understanding of the wider political and military dynamics that spurred France into reclaiming its colonies in Southeast Asia, some time should be given to providing an overview of events taking place slightly further to the west of Vietnam, in Laos and in Cambodia. The two following sections start with a brief presentation of each country before moving on to the presentation of two separate chronologies using 1945 as a starting point.

A landlocked country in Southeast Asia, Laos lies at the centre of the Indochinese Peninsula. In 1945, it was bordered by Burma and China to the northwest, by Cambodia and Thailand to southeast, west, and southwest respectively, and Vietnam lay to its east. Historically, Laos was divided into three different kingdoms after the breakup of the unified kingdom of Lan Xang (1353–1707). The creation of the kingdoms of Luang Prabang, Vientiane and Champassak, followed this split but in 1893, the three different territories were reunited by the imposition of a protectorate by France. Henceforth, Laos was part of France's Second Colonial Empire, an empire constructed from 1830 with the conquest of Algiers, Algeria.

Laos, 1945

9 March
After Japan invaded Indochina, French authorities created a Franco-Laotian resistance whose members included Prince Boun Oum of Champassak. Serving as a lieutenant, Boun Oum took part in guerrilla operations led by French paratroopers to retake the city of Paksé on southern Laos in the summer of 1945.

16 March
A week after the Japanese invasion, Boun Oum's brother, Prince Savang Vat Thana, ordered a general uprising against the invaders.

Unlike Bao Dai in Vietnam and Norodom Sihanouk in Cambodia, his father, King Sisavang Vong, first refused to declare his country's independence from France. However, under pressure from Laotian Prime Minister Phetsarath Rattanavongsa, on 8 April 1945 Sisavang gave in to Japanese demands. At the same time, Phetsarath created a communist inspired, anti-French, nationalist movement called the Lao Issara. Soon this movement evolved into the Pathet Lao and shortly it received military support from an army created by Phetsarath's half-brother, Prince Souphanouvong, or the 'Red Prince' due to his affiliations with communism. The Pathet Lao became an ally of the Viet Minh.

5 April
Japanese forces occupy Luang Phrabang.

8 April
King Sisavang declares Laotian independence.

17 July
The Potsdam Declaration gives China the authority to disarm Japanese forces north of the 16th Parallel, while Great Britain performs the same role south of this line.
15 August
Surrender of Japanese forces in Indochina.

30 August
Sisavang declares that Laos is once more a French protectorate.

1 September
Phetsarath declares that the Franco-Thai Treaty of March 1941 (which saw Laos cede the Sayaboury and Champassak to Thailand) is null and void.

2 September
The surrender of all Japanese forces in the Pacific. The Laotian Nation Party is created in Vientiane.

September
Chinese forces begin to disarm Japanese forces in Indochina.

September
Prince Boun Oum invites French troops to return to Paksé.

September
Phetsarath declares the creation of the Lao Kingdom. It replaces the Luang Prabang Kingdom and he announces formation of the Lao Issara government with himself as prime minister.

4 October
Phetsarath calls for the international recognition of the new regime.

October
France pushes King Sisavang to dismiss Phetsarath.

12 October
The Lao Issara declares the independence of Laos. It creates a 'House of People's Representatives' whose members include Phetsarath's brother (Prince Souvanna Phouma), his half-brother (Prince Souphanouvong), and Katay Don Sasorith, one of the chief spokesmen of the Laotian nationalist movement.

14 October
The inauguration of the Lao Issara government.

17 October
Troops of China's 93rd Division arrive in Luang Prabang.

20 October
King Sisavang is dethroned by the Lao Issara government. Phetsarath is appointed Head of State.

30 October
The Pathet Lao and the Viet Minh conclude a military agreement.

1 November
After meeting Ho Chi Minh, Prince Souphanouvong is appointed Minister of Defence in the new Laotian government.

Laos, 1946

28 February
The Franco-Chinese Accords see Nationalist Chinese forces begin their withdrawal from Indochina.

March
Souphanouvong organises his forces to fight against the French.

6 March
Signing of the Sainteny-Ho Chi Minh agreements which see French forces arrive in Haiphong.

17 March
Savannakhet in western Laos is occupied by French forces.

18 March
French forces under general Leclerc enter Hanoi.

21 March
Souphanouvong orders that a popular uprising against French rule should take place in Thakhek, a town in south central Laos lying on the Mekong River. Under the command of Jean Boucher de Crevecoeur, troops of the 5e RIC and of the *Forces du Laos* supported by artillery and French fighter aircraft (see *chapter 5*) carried out short, but intensive, urban warfare on a joint Pathet Lao-Viet Minh enemy. Souphanouvong was injured and over 400 enemy soldiers were killed with the loss of some 250 men fighting under French colours. In the face of this defeat, most members of the Lao Issara fled to Thailand where they remained until autumn 1949.

23 April
King Sisavang Vong claims back his throne.

24 April
French troops enter and occupy Vientiane.

26 April
A new government led by Prince Kindavong comes to power.

13 May
French troops seize Luang Prabang.

30 May
The Kuomintang leave Tonkin.

1 June
Cochinchina unilaterally declares its independence as an 'Autonomous Republic'.

10 June
The KMT begins to leave Hanoi.

12 June
Ho Chi Minh arrives in Biarritz as part of peace talks with France.

27 June
Ho Chi Minh meets representatives of the French government in Paris.

July
Souphanouvong leaves Bangkok for Hanoi for discussions with Ho Chi Minh and other North Vietnamese leaders.

17 August
French and Laotian representatives reach an agreement whereby Laos becomes an autonomous entity inside the Indochinese Union.

26 August
Prince Boun Oum renounces his right to the throne of Champassak leaving Sisavang as the ruler of all Laos.

14 September
Signing of a *modus vivendi* between Marius Moutet and Ho Chi Minh.

15 November
An agreement is signed in Washington DC that sees France and Thailand hand back territories taken from Laos in 1941.

23 November
French warships bomb Haiphong.

15 December
Laotian parliamentary elections are held.

16 December
Celebrations are held in honour of the reintegration of the Laotian provinces of Sayaboury and Champassak.

19 December
Battle of Hanoi and Tonkin uprising.

Laos, 1947

February
Souphanouvong makes a failed attempt to defeat Franco-Laotian forces in northern Laos.

15 March
The Laotian parliament votes in favour of the new Laotian constitution.

11 May
Laos becomes a constitutional monarchy within the French Union.

21 November
The opening of the first Laotian National Assembly.

25 November
Prince Souvannarath is appointed as head of the Royal government of Laos.

28 November
General Leclerc is killed in a plane crash near Colomb-Bèchard, French Algeria.

23 December
Both Laos and Cambodia request to join the French Union.

Laos, 1948

24 April
First opening of the King's Council.

16 August
The Laotian constitution is put forward for revision.

Laos, 1949

16 April
Souphanouvong is dismissed from the Lao Issara movement.

19 July
France and Laos sign a provisional agreement in Paris whereby Laos becomes an associate member of the French Union.

13 October
The Lao Issara movement is disbanded.

Laotian pro-French military Forces, 1941–1949

Although French colonial authorities feared that Laotians did not possess the necessary military attributes to make up battalions of *tirailleurs*, this situation changed in 1941 when Admiral Decoux first allowed Laotians to serve within Vietnamese units. This paved the way for the creation of the mainly Laotian 2e *Compagnie* of the 4/10e *Régiment d'Infanterie Colonial* (4/10e RMIC) based at Dong Hene. A second company was formed in Vientiane in 1942 – the 25e *Compagnie* of the 4/10e RMIC – and was based at Vientiane. However, companies of around 4,000 men in total, retreated to China following the Japanese invasion of March 1945.

In October 1945, King Sisavang Vong encouraged these men (mainly from the Hmong tribe) to join the French Terrestrial Forces in the Far East (FTEO). Leclerc accepted them as *Bataillions de Chasseurs Laotiens* (BCLs) and by 1 July 1949, eight BCLs were stationed in Vientiane and other major urban areas of Laos such as Phongsaly. Other Laotian units included the 2e, 3e, 4e and 6e *Commandos Laotiens* drawn from the ranks of the BCLs, as well as a parachute company trained at Thakhek and Vientiane. This was the 6e *Commando Laotien* (6th Laotian Commando) created on 16 August 1946 and whose job was to relieve the 5e REI which was based in the Sam Neau region of Laos from June that year.

In September 1946, the 6th Laotian Commando joined the 6e *Bataillon de Chasseurs Laotiens* (6e BCL) and elements of the *Bataillon Thai* (Thai Batallion) in the *Groupement Quilichini*, the name given to

Troops of the Laotian Bataillon de chasseurs line up in Vientiane circa 1947. Although the rank and file consisted of locally recruited Laotians, indigenous units such as this were commanded by French officers. (Author's collection)

French forces based in Yunnan and commanded by General Robert Quilichini.

By July 1948, just over 4,000 Laotian regulars were members of the FTEO (a number that rose to 7,762 in 1952). These regulars were reinforced by auxiliaries and other irregular forces acting as local militias. Estimates put the number of these irregulars as few as 1,000, but as many as 2,500 in 1948.[1] In that year, it was decided that they would be organised into *Compagnies Légères de Supplétifs Militaires* (CLSM) or light companies of military auxiliaries). Gradually and from February 1950, all Laotian military forces would form the National Laotian Army (LNA).

As for French regulars based in Laos during the First Indochinese War, they mainly served as the officers of the Laotian units or as officers in the Laotian gendarmerie created in May 1946. The role of the gendarmerie was to enforce law and order in different provinces and to reinforce Laotian and French regulars if, and when, needed.

Cambodia, 1946

Cambodia in the nineteenth century was similar to Laos in that it was ruled over by a dynastic monarchy. King Ang Duong was the country's monarch around the time France began to make commercial incursions into the heart of Southeast Asia (1850s) and on his death in 1860, he was succeeded by his son, Norodom the First. Forced into exile in Siam by his brother, Si Votha a year later, in 1863 Norodom accepted France's proposal to set up a protectorate that would see his return to Cambodia and put an end to the war between the different factions of the Cambodian royal family. French forces intervened in Cambodia in 1867 following another insurrection intended to oust Norodom. To quell the fighting, France annexed the country in 1884. Three years later, Cambodia became a member of the newly created Indochinese Union.

As in the rest of Indochina, the early 1930s saw the growth of opposition to French rule and the emergence of nationalist parties claiming independence. Cambodia was no different and 1940 saw the birth of the Khmer Issarak. Based in Bangkok, the movement received support from the Thai government and in return, the Khmer Issarak sent guerrilla groups to assist Thailand in the Franco-Thai War.

Whereas British troops entered Phnom Penh on 8 October of that year, two changes made to the composition of the Cambodian government led to the creation of the country's first national army. Firstly, the nationalist revolutionary and Prime Minister Son Ngoc Thanh was arrested by the French on 12 October 1945 and secondly, he was replaced by Prince Monireth five days later. Monireth suggested to the French that he raise an

indigenous army to fill the vacuum left by the Japanese to counter increasing civil and political unrest in the country.

This suggestion led to the creation of Cambodia's first national army formed using former members of the *Bataillon de Tirailleurs Cambodgiens* and to the opening of an officer-cadet training academy on 1 January 1946. The standing of the Cambodian army was strengthened through the Franco-Cambodian *modus vivendi* signed on 4 January 1946 but although the agreement gave Cambodia internal autonomy, French advisers were placed inside

The insignia of the Khmer Royal Army. (Author's collection)

BCK troops armed with the MAS-36 bolt-action rifle. Also note the Palladium 'Pampa' boots first issued to the French Foreign Legion in 1947. (Author's collection)

the Cambodian Ministry of Defence and French forces were given the responsibility of maintaining order in the country.

The presence of French forces led to Issarak guerrillas attacking a hotel lodging French Army officers on 7 April 1946 and four months later at Siem Reap, they killed seven French soldiers. In an effort to stabilise the Cambodian context, France and Cambodian officials then signed the Franco-Khmer Military Convention of 20 November 1946. The agreement was significant in that it established the role and organisation of the Cambodian military, the Khmer Royal Army (ARK), as well as confirming that Cambodia was an autonomous state within the newly created French Union. The missions of the ARK (*Armée Royale Khmère* in French) were to maintain order within Cambodia using territorial units, but it was also called upon to help safeguard the integrity of the French Union by placing its military units at the disposal of the French High Commissioner.

However, the position of these Cambodian 'mobile reserve' units stationed in Indochina depended on a mutual decision made by both authorities. Four thousand Khmer soldiers would form the territorial guard while another 4,000 would serve within the CEFEO as the mobile reserve (*réserve mobile*). The training of ARK forces was entrusted to the French Army and three days later, the first entirely Cambodian regular unit was raised in Phnom Penh. This 1e *Bataillon de Chasseurs Khmères* (1e BCK) or 1st Khmer Rifle Battalion, was formed from elements of the *Garde Indigène* ('Indigenous Guard') and the *Régiment de Tirailleurs Cambodgiens* (RTC), or Cambodian Rifle Regiment. A second rifle battalion, the 2e *Bataillon de Chasseurs Khmères* (2e BCK) was formed using auxiliaries (*supplétifs*) and was created in December 1946 in Kracheh, in eastern Cambodia. In January 1947, both battalions became part of the mobile reserve.

By 1947, opposition to French rule involved diverse groups – some communist inspired, some not – intent on gaining full independence for Cambodia. The Khmer Issarak began to receive training and weapons provided by the Viet Minh early in this year as Ho Chi Minh saw Cambodia as a base from where attacks could be made against the French in southern Vietnam. In the face of mounting insecurity and Viet Minh activity, the Cambodian government made a concerted effort to recruit and by January 1947, its numbers grew to approximately 4,000 of the 8,000 initially forecasted.

Two-thirds of these forces served in a gendarmerie commanded by French officers (*Régiment Mixte du Cambodge*) while the remainder served in the first and second battalions of Cambodian riflemen, the 1e and 2e *Bataillons de Chasseurs Khmères*. Cambodia's military context improved with the raising of the 3rd BCK at Takéo in southern Cambodia in August 1948. Half of these forces were stationed elsewhere within Indochina by the end of 1949. As for French forces based permanently in Cambodia from 1945, the *Commando/Groupement Blindé du Cambodge* (GBC) was among the first French units to return to Indochina. On 15 September 1946, the GBC became the 8esc/5e *Régiment de Cuirassiers* (8/5e RC).

Thai Battalions

As mentioned previously, in September 1946 the French command decided to create the Thai Autonomous Battalion to relieve troops based near the Laotian border with China. A second Thai Battalion was created in July 1947 and a third in October 1949. The first battalion was initially made up of five companies of *fusiliers voltigeurs*, or skirmish units, but this was reduced to three plus a commando unit, upon the creation of the second battalion. Commanded by French soldiers, the Thai units were trained for jungle fighting. They took part in operations *Geneviève* and *Bénédicte* in September – October 1947, two operations that preceded or coincided with Operation *Léa*.

5

THE FRENCH AIR FORCE (AND OTHER AVIATION) IN INDOCHINA

When considering the *Armée de l'Air* (French Air Force) in Indochina from 1945–1949, to say that it was ill-prepared for any major conflict – let alone the type it was facing – is an understatement. The most immediate reason for a lack of preparedness is that the Second World War brought the domestic production of aircraft to a standstill, but even in the years preceding France's occupation by Nazi Germany, the air force found its development hamstrung by wider military and political considerations. Indeed, despite increasing evidence that air power was an increasingly effective tool in an ever-evolving form of war, French Army generals stuck to the notion that the role of aircraft was merely to act as spotters and to guide artillery fire in a static type of warfare similar to the First World War.

It should come as no surprise to learn that the French Air Force was created just four years before the outbreak of war with Nazi Germany. At the time of its creation, France was traversing one of the most tumultuous political periods in its modern history and was on the brink of civil war. A succession of different governments attempted to redress a troubled industrial context – as well as addressing social issues – but even by 1938, French manufacturers were primarily manufacturing aircraft that were already becoming obsolete and that were few in numbers. A good illustration was the Morane-Saulnier MS.405. In 1934, this single-seater fighter was selected to form the backbone of France's burgeoning air power, but first deliveries only began in late 1938. By then, the British were manufacturing the more powerful Hawker Hurricanes and Germans, the Messerschmitt Bf.109s. Arguably, the MS.406 was armed with a gun which British and German fighters only received later.

Moreover, the Dewoitine D.520, which was in production by 1939, was outmatching both the Hurricane and Bf.109: however, both French types were deployed along a much poorer doctrine than that of the Luftwaffe and later the same year, the British also pressed the brand new Supermarine Spitfire into production.

Better aircraft were in the production pipeline – the Dewoitine D.520 or the Amiot 354 bomber, for example – but as war with Germany became more likely, the French government found itself obliged to place orders abroad for combat aircraft such as the Curtis

Escadre, Escadron, or Escadrille? Unit Designations of the French Air Force

The French Air Force (Armée de l'Air) traces its origins back to 1909, when the French Army established the *Aéronaturique Militaire* (Aeronautical Service) as one of its corps-level sub-branches. During the First World War, the Aeronautical Service was organised into regiments, which consisted of flights – *Escadrille*. The AdA was officially established on 1 April 1933 and retained flights as its core units, but replaced the regimental structure with wings, each of which was composed of three groups: each group had three flights on average.

From 1939, the wings generally adopted the structure of two groups (*groupe*), each of three flights: the squadron-structure (*escadron*) was only introduced in 1949, at the end of the period covered in this volume.

As of the period 1945-1949, the most important organisation element was the wing – *escadre* – the purpose of which was identified by suffix in the designation. For example: *Escadre de Chasse* (EC) was the fighter wing, *Escadre de Bombardement* (EB) was a bomber wing. The initials were followed by a single- or double-digit suffix. Each *escadre* consisted of up to three groups – *groupe* (G) – the designation of which contained a number and a name of a province or a city. For example: *Group de Chase* (GC) was a fighter group, *Group de Bombardement* (GC) was a bomber group. In written documentation, primary difference between *escadre* and *groupe* was the use of Arabic digits to designate the former and Latin digits to designate the latter. For example: EC.2/3 Champagne stood for 2nd Fighter Wing, 3rd Group, named after the province of Champagne, while GC.II/1 stood for 2nd Fighter Group, 1st Flight.

The flights (*escuadrilles*) remained important because throughout all this time, they remained the actual core element of all flying units. Usually there were three within each group: the mass of these drew their names, traditions, designations, insignias and other regalia from flights established during the First World War (foremost those equipped with Spad aircraft, thus wearing the designation 'SPA'). While explaining stories of single flights is well beyond the scope of this book, sufficient to say that the AdA developed the tradition of applying the flight-insignia on one side and the wing- and/or group-insignia on the other side of the fin of its aircraft.

Hawk 75A, the Martin 167 and the Douglas DB-7 twin-engined bomber. Many were not delivered and the French Air Force had to face the Nazis with what aircraft it had.

The shortfall in more modern aircraft did not mean, however, that the *Armée de l'Air* lacked experience: some: some 15 had taken part in the Battle of France; some had fought in the Battle of Britain and in the USSR as members of the Free French Air Force (FAFL), while others had flown a mixture of aircraft under the auspices of the Vichy Air Force. By the time this unit had been disbanded, French airmen were undergoing training on Hurricanes or Handley Page Halifaxes, while instruction in fighter tactics was being given at training centres in Tunisia and Morocco.

This experience and training paved the way for operations in support of the landings in the south of France in August 1944 and the formation of a fully qualified and professional outfit. Nonetheless, problems with the production of aircraft still existed and this made the task of effectively confronting the Viet Minh far more difficult than it could have been should the requisite equipment have been available.

The French Air Force in Indochina, circa May 1940

Commanded by Colonel Devèze, in terms of equipment, Vichy France's air forces in Indochina in 1941 suffered more restrictions than those representing Marshal Petain in the North African campaign against Great Britain. That said, what aerial forces it did possess were organised following the structure and hierarchy of any traditional air force. At the head of the organisation was the *Commandement de l'Air en Indochine* (CAI) which oversaw operations in three zones: Tonkin and north Laos (ZOTON, Hanoi); Annam and Central/Southern Laos (ZOAL, Hué); Cochinchina and Cambodia (ZOCOC, Saigon). In total, the French Air Force and the French Naval Aviation operated 337 aircraft, and another 100 were operated by the American Volunteer Group (AVG). Not counting the Regional Patrol aircraft, Indochina's defence forces could deploy 244 frontline aircraft when including the AVG squadrons and the eight Lockheed Hudsons of Fleet E29.

In 1942, the Vichy Air Force in Indochina underwent a major reorganisation. Two units of the newly created *Groupe Aérien Nord Indochine* (GANI) were based at Tong in Tonkin and used the following:

Groupement Mixte 1: Farman 221s and Potez 542s.
Groupement Mixte 2: Potez 25s and MS.406s.

The *Groupe Aérien Centre Indochine* (GACI) consisted of an observation unit based at Bach Mai in Tonkin, using Potez 25s; and the *Groupe Aérien Mixte 4* based at Dong Hoi in Annam and Vat Chay in Cambodia using Potez 25s and Loire 130s. By December 1942, the number of aircraft available had decreased significantly and the Vichy Air Force possessed three Farman 221s, two Potez 542s, 18 Potez 25 TOEs, and seven Loire 130s.

The Fighter Aircraft of the Force Aérienne Française d'Extrême-Orient (FAFEO)

Fighter Squadrons

1e *Escadron de chasse* (1e EC). November 1945 – August 1946. Consisting of two fighter groups: *Groupe de Chasse I/7 'Provence'* (GC I/7), and GC II/7 'Nice'. Each GC consisted of two smaller units called SPAs, an acronym for *Société de Production des Aéroplanes*. The acronym was adopted by air units during the First World War and originally denoted that a particular fighter squadron was operating SPAD aircraft (*Société de Production des Aéroplanes Deperdussin*). After the First World War, the term was used by units no matter what type of aircraft used. Each SPA wore individual insignia.

Based at Friedrichshafen, Germany during the summer of 1945, the 1e EC boarded the US Navy's SS *Georgetown Victory* and SS *American Victory* at Marseilles on 2 November. Arriving in Saigon on 26 November, the personnel of the fighter group then travelled to their base at Tan Son Nhut airfield to await delivery of a consignment of Supermarine Spitfire LF.Mk IXs and HF.Mk IX supplied by Great Britain. The delivery delayed due to a strike by British dockers, the FAFEO trained on a miscellany of Spitfire Mk VIIIs, de Havilland Mosquito PR.Mk XVI and PR.Mk XXXIV loaned by the RAF's Nos. 273 and 684 squadrons also based at Tan Son Nhut.[2] GT II/7 carried out its first carried out its first reconnaissance mission on 12 December, and on 15 December it provided air support for the

Table 5: Organisation of French Air Force in Franco-Thai War, September 1940 [1]				
Unit	Type of aircraft	Number of aircraft	Base	Commander
Groupe Aérien Autonome 41 (GAA)				
Esc. R 1/41	Potez 25	9	Pursat (Cambodia)	Lt Adam
EB 2/41	Farman 221	4	Tong (Tonkin)	Cne Penchinat
Groupe Aérien Autonome 42 (GAA)				
Esc. R 1/42	Potez 25	10	Pursat (Cambodia)	Cne Minard
EB 2/42	Potez 542	6	Tan Son Nhut (Cochinchina)	Cne Jacquelin
Groupe Aérien Mixte 595 (GAM)				
EO 1/595	Potez 25	7	Dong-Hoï (Annam)	Cdt Maynard
Groupe Aérien Mixte 596 (GAM)				
EO 1/596	Potez 25	8	Tourane/Da Nang (Annam)	Cne Bodin
Esc. 1/CBS	Loire 130 CAMS 37 & 55	4	Cat-Lai (Cochinchina)	Cne Michel
Commandement des Bases du Sud (Southern Bases Command)				
Esc. 1/CBS	Loire 130 CAMS 37 CAMS 35	8, 2 and 2 respectively	Cat-Lai (Cochinchina)	Cne Michel
Aéronautique Navale				
Esc. HS6	Loire 130 Gourdou-Leseurre 832 Potez 452	2, 3 and 3 respectively	Cat-Lai	LV Gaxotte
Missions recorded during war with Thailand				
Unit	Day missions		Night missions	
Esc. R 1/41	1		-	
Esc. B 2/41	-		15	
Esc. R 1/42	15		-	
Esc. B 2/42	1		14	
EC 2/595	10		-	
EO 1/596	114		5	
EC 2/596	42		-	
Esc. 1/CBS	4		19	
Potez 631C	4		1	
Aircraft after war with Thailand				
Type	Available for service		Unavailable for service	Total
MS 406	14		5	19
Farman 221	3		-	3
Potez 542	3		1	4
Potez 631	-		3	
Potez 25	34		20	54
Loire 130	9		3	12
Total	63		32	95

The Morane-Saulnier MS.406 was a French fighter aircraft developed and manufactured by Morane-Saulnier from 1938. It was one of only two French fighters designed to exceed a speed of over 250 mph (400km/h), the other being the Potez 630. While the MS.406s here line up in France and wear French Air Force camouflage of the time, those used under the Vichy government had red and yellow stripes added to the engine cowling and tail unit. The main markings included a thin, yellow outline and the roundel was displayed in six positions. (WW2Aircraft.net)

The Farman 221 was produced by Farman Aviation Works, one of France's oldest aircraft manufacturers. An aircraft that was used from 1936 by the *Armée de l'Air*, the aircraft featured hand-operated turrets for the three gunner's stations. The aircraft were powered by four Gnome-Rhône 14-cylinder engines. (WW2Aircraft.net)

Potez 540 was a multi-role aircraft from the mid-1930s. Developed as a private venture, it was deployed by the French Air Force as bomber, transport, for long-range reconnaissance, and for paratrooper training. Most were either retired or destroyed by the end of 1943. (Author's collection)

GM and the 9e DIC during operations around the Plain of Reeds.[3]

If a resolution had been found through the supplying of British aircraft, the FEFEO was still faced with serious shortages that put any operational plans its commanders had in mind, in jeopardy. The British did put forward another plan however, which consisted of handing the French a list of aircraft that had been abandoned by the Japanese as they fled Cambodia. Though the list was rejected at first, the French General Staff soon realised that they were short of options and began to give closer attention to the proposal. Included on the list were not just aircraft captured by the 'Gremlin Task Force', but spares, weapons, and ammunition; just what France needed to constitute a temporary air force while other solutions were found.

Summary of missions flown by the EC.1 to August 1946

• December 1945: Spitfires of the 2/7 strafe VM guerrillas around the Plain of Reeds.

• 28 December 1945: Machine gunning of a village.

• 21 January 1946: Two Ki-43 'Oscars' from 1/7 depart Tan Son Nhut on a leaflet-dropping mission. The mission is aborted at the last minute and transferred over to the DC-3s of the *Groupe de Transport*.

• From 23 January to 2 February, four Spitfire Mk 8s from 2/7 were transferred to Nha Trang while four Mk 8s from 1/7 were deployed to Seno airfield in Laos. Three Spitfire Mk 9s were delivered to Tan Son Nhut.

• 1 March 1946: From this date, elements of 1/7 are sent to Tonkin and carrying out low altitude runs to intimidate Chinese units and to persuade them to respect terms laid out in the Potsdam Declaration. This month sees 2/7 send four aircraft to Seno, Laos where it

The Potez 542 was a variant of the Potez 540. Manufactured by French company Potez from 1932, it served with the *Armée de l'Air* as a reconnaissance bomber. The Potez 542 was powered by 720 hp Lorraine 12Hfrs Pétrel V-12 engines. (passionair1940.fr)

The Loire 130 was a French flying boat built by Loire Aviation of St. Nazaire. Its service mainly carried out aboard most battleships and cruisers of the French Navy, a good number survived the war and served in French colonies until the early 1950s. (passionair.fr)

• May 1946: Spitfires clear the sectors around the Plain of Reeds (Thap Muoi Plain) northwest of the Mekong Delta. After these operations, it is noticed that the tropical climate is causing the tyres of the aircraft to deteriorate quickly and that the aircraft's Merlin glycol-cooled engines became overheated and stressed due to flying exclusively at low altitude. The two GCs often operated alongside seaplanes used by the French Navy for duties round coastal regions and the number of aircraft used in operations depended on their type: two aircraft for short patrols, for example. Replaced by the 2nd Fighter Squadron in July 1946, the 1st Squadron left for Friedrichshafen in August 1946 before being transferred to Oran, Algeria.

EC 2 (July 1946 – October 1947)

Made up of Fighter Group I/2 'Cigognes' (GC I/2) and GC III/2 (subsequently GC II/2) 'Alsace'. Designated to take the place of the 1e EC, the personnel of the 2e EC left Friedrichshafen in occupied Germany at the end of June 1946 to board the ocean liner *Pasteur* on 16 July. Arriving in Indochina on 3 August, the 2e EC was based at Tan Son Nhut where it took over the Spitfire LF.Mk IX left left by its predecessors.

Summary of missions carried out by 2 EC

• The first sorties were made on 7 August accompanied by crews of the 1e EC and consisted of area reconnaissance. The next day, a patrol group from GC III/2 was sent to Cambodia to deal with a series of incidents involving the Khmer Issarek along the Thai-Cambodian border.

• In late August 1946, one section of 1/2 (SPA 3) was deployed to Cambodia where it operated out of Pochentong airfield in Phnom Penh while the other section (SPA 103) was sent to Gia Lam in Tonkin. Operation *Oméga* of December 1946 sees Spitfires from 3/2 sent to Paksé, Laos and Nha Trang.

• 19 December 1946: SPA 103 provides air support near Bac Ninh and attacks a concentration of VM forces near Phu Lang Thuong. SPA 3 is called back from Cambodia to provide support for SPA 103 as trouble in Tonkin continues.

takes part in the Battle of Thakhek on 21 March. Here, Pathet Lao guerrillas supported by the VM had taken over the city in a show of demonstration against French rule. The attacks involved commandos from the 5e RIC and the 1er BCL.

• 7 April 1946: four aircraft from GC I/7 bomb Chinese positions at Dien Bien Phu in retaliation for attacks made on the French Army.

• 19 April 1946: 13 aircraft take part in a bombing mission over the Bien Hoa region.

• 25 April 1946: 'Provence' provides air support for troops marching towards Hué and Vientiane, while 'Nice' intervened in the Camau sector following Viet Minh attacks against landing craft.

Supermarine Spitfire Mk IXs pictured at Tan Son Nhut airfield, *circa* January 1946. (Author's collection)

Insignia of the EC 2/595. The unit was created in September 1939 at Bach Mai. (Author's collection)

The insignia of the EC 2/596. (Author's collection)

Chief Petty Officer Châtel (right) at Dong Hene airfield, October 1940. A number of naval pilots were seconded to help out the *Armée de l'Air*. (warfarehistorian)

- January 1947: Nha Trang becomes the main base of operations for 3/2 with detachments also operating in South Annam and Laos.
- 24 May: The rising waters of the Red River at this time of the year see GC I/2 leave Gia Lam for Cat Bi (Haiphong) until mid-June. Intelligence reports that Ho Chi Minh has set up HQ in Phu Minh near Hanoi, so from 26 May to 12 June GC I/2 flies reconnaissance missions over the area.
- June: GC I/2 bombs Phu Minh before the arrival of grounds troops during Operation *Marcel*. The operation lasts from 8 to 23 June with the objective of clearing the area around Fai Fo (now Hoi An). GC III/2 commits six aircraft from Tourane and over two days it carries out 32 sorties. It destroys around 50 junks suspected of carrying VM supplies as well as a VM communications transmitter.
- 29 June to 7 July: GC III/2 patrols an area some 500kms south of Hanoi and operates out of a makeshift airfield at Dong Ho. Here, it provides air support for the 3/23 RIC. GC III/2 becomes GC II/2 on 1 July.
- 31 August – 2 September: The 2e EC attacks VM positions at Quang Nam and Ha Tranh (south of Tourane) and destroys a VM radio transmitter. A second VM transmitter is destroyed in the Ba Na Hills near Tourane.
- October 1947: The 2e EC leaves Indochina for Koblenz, Germany.

The GC I/3 'Corse' (January to June 1947)
Composition: SPA 69 and SPA 88

GC I /3 was firstly sent to Rabat in Morocco in November 1946 to receive training on the De Haviland DH. 98 Mosquito, then it was transferred to Indochina on 16 January 1947 where it operated 10 Mosquito FB.Mk 6 fighter-bombers. Seen as better adapted to conditions than the Spitfire Mk 9, the FB.Mk 6 was armed with four Browning 7.62 machine guns in its upper nose, and four 20mm Hispano Mk 2 cannons below. Although they were never used, the Mosquito could also be adapted to carry RP-3 (Rocket Projectile 3 inch) air-to-ground rockets. Among the GC I/3's first missions was the securing of areas to the west of Saigon in March 1947 and the group was to carry out 345 sorties during which it amassed 740 flying hours. It dropped 84 tonnes of bombs and used 150,000

What was the Gremlin Task Force?

As is the case in any conflict, the obtaining and subsequent study of weapons used by the enemy is integral to the development of defence mechanisms that can be used against the weapons in question. The context provided by the Second World War was, naturally, no different and in early 1943, the Allies created Technical Air Intelligence Units (TAIUs) solely for the purpose of learning as much about enemy weapons and equipment as possible. The first TAIU was set up in Australia as a joint operation between the USAAF, the US Navy and the Royal Australian Air Force (RAAF) and soon it integrated members of the Directorate of Intelligence, HQ Allied forces, who were putting together a system that would enable them to identify Japanese aircraft by using individual codenames. A second TAIU known as the ATAIU-SEA (Allied TAIU, South East Asia) was set up in Calcutta later in 1943 by the RAF and the USAAF, while other TAIUs were created to cover the South West Pacific Area (TAIU-SWPA), the Pacific Ocean Area (TAIU-POA), and nationalist China (TAIU-China).

By the end of 1945, the ATAIU-SEA based in Singapore had managed to log almost every type of aircraft used by the Japanese in Burma or Cambodia. Some aircraft destined for study by the ATAIU-SEA still remained in Saigon, and these would appear on the list handed to the French in January. In the meantime, with the RAF also short on aircraft (particularly bombers and transport aircraft), Air Chief Marshal Sir Walter Cheshire decided that he would put the captured air force to good use and form an air unit called the Gremlin Task Force (GTF). Created in October 1945, though the GTF was commanded by Squadron Leader H.F. McNab assisted by other RAF officers, many of its crew members were former pilots and technicians of the IJAAF.

The aircraft, themselves, served a variety of different roles right u to the disbandment of the GTF in February 1946 when they became the property of the French. Some like Ki-36 'Ida', the Ki-51 'Sonia', the Ki-46 'Dinah', and the Ki-48 'Lily' were used for photoreconnaissance, while others such as the Ki-21 'Sally', the Ki-54 'Hickory', or the Ki-57 'Topsy', were used for troop transport. During January 1946, the GTF flew 408 sorties over 810 flying hours and transported 2,200 passengers as well as 228 tonnes of freight to destinations in Cambodia, Singapore, and Thailand.[4]

This Mitsubishi G4M 'Betty' was just one of the Japanese aircraft serviced and used by the ATAIU-SEA after the surrender of Japan. Nicknamed the 'flying Zippo' due to its tendency to catch fire easily, this bomber could be armed with a Type 91 Torpedo (Kai-3), and its standard armament were four Arisaka Type 92 machine guns and a 20mm Type 99 rear-mounted cannon. This photo clearly shows the (rudimentary) markings of the ATAIU and the RAF roundel. (Author's collection

The Mitsubishi A6M 'Zero' was another aircraft put into service by the ATAIU and used by the GTF. Designated as a Navy Type 0 long-range carrier fighter, it gained a fearsome reputation due to its manoeuvrability. Though not as fast as the Supermarine Spitfire, the 'Zero' could out-turn the British fighter. Many were used in the attack on Pearl Harbour. (Author's collection)

Japanese Aircraft used by the Gremlin Task Force

- 4 Mitsubishi Ki-57 II 'Topsy'
- 4 Mitsubishi Ki-21 'Sally'
- Tachikawa Ki-55/Ki-36 'Ida' (number not known)
- Mitsubishi Ki-46 'Dinah' (number not known)
- 1 Kawasaki Ki-48 'Lily'
- Tachikawa Ki-54 'Hickory' (number not known)
- 1 Kawasaki Ki-61 'Tony'
- Mitsubishi Ki-67 'Peggy' (number not known)
- 2 Nakajima L2D2 Ki-16 'Tabby'

rounds of ammunition but faced with a shortage of spare parts for the Mosquito, the group was forced to return to Morocco on 10 June 1947. On 1 July 1947 the group was renamed GC I/6 and would return to Indochina in March 1950.

The Japanese Aircraft of the French Air Force

It would be wholly incorrect to say that the *Armée de l'Air* (AdA) relied solely on the GTF or the ATAUI for its aircraft. In fact, during 1946–1947, the AdA was operating no less than 88 different types of French, British, US, Belgian, German, Russian and Japanese aircraft.[5] Nevertheless, this section will describe to what extent the former aircraft of the IJA, the IJN and the IJAF, were deployed by the French in the early years of the Indochinese conflict. It should also be mentioned that although the AdA's fleet of Japanese aircraft was bolstered by the arrival in February 1946 of aircraft formerly used by the GTF, GC I/17 and GC II/17 were already operating nearly 30 Nakajima Ki-43 'Oscars' from Tan Son Nhut and Phnom Penh.

In addition to the GTF aircraft listed previously, the ATAIU provided the AdA with operational examples of the following:

- Nakajima A6M2-N 'Rufe'
- Aichi E13A 'Jake'
- Mitsubishi G4M 'Betty'
- Yokosuka MXY7 'Baka'
- Mitsubishi A6M2 and A6M5 'Zero'
- Mitsubishi J2M 'Jack'
- Kokusai Ki-85 'Cypress'

Two of these types were of particular interest to the AdA (the Ki-43 and the Ki-54) as they could be used as transport and liaison aircraft in expectation of six Douglas C-47s operated by the French *Escadrille de Marche d'Extrême-Orient* (EMEO) – GMEO or GMTEO from December 1945 – that were still based at Jessore, India and would not arrive in Indochina until January 1946.[6] More aircraft were left as scrap by the Japanese at Bien Hoa, and French technicians were able to put some of them back into service. They were as follows:

- Ki-43 'Oscars' (6 operational)
- 3 A6M2 'Zeros' (1 operational)
- 2 Nakajima Ki-44 Shoki 'Tojos' (non-operational)
- 1 Ki-21 IIb 'Sally' (non-operational)
- 2 Kokusai Ki-59 'Theresas' (1 operational)
- 3 Ki-54 'Hickorys' (1 operational)
- 1 Ki-61 'Tony' (non-operational)
- 7 E13A1 'Jakes' (4 operational)
- 8 A6M2-N 'Rufes' (4 operational)

The Kokusai Ki-86 was a version of the Swedish-designed Bücker Bü 131 Jungmann produced under licence for the IJA. Primarily used as a trainer, this single bay biplane was later adapted for use as a bomber. Powered by the 110hp Hitachi (HA-47) 4-cylinder and air-cooled engine, here we see ATAIU personnel and Japanese pilots inspecting the aircraft. (Imperial War Museum)

A Mitsubishi Ki-46 'Dinah' in French service. This model was pictured flying out of Tan Son Nhut in February 1946. (Author's collection)

The Tachikawa Ki-54 'Hickory' was mainly used for crew training but was used for other purposes after the Second World War. This one is pictured in French service at Tan Son Nhut in early 1946. (Author's collection)

NB. Examples of the Mitsubishi Ki-30 'Ann'; the Mitsubishi Ki-51 'Sonia'; and the Nakajima Ki-34 'Thora' also ended up in French service though their source is unknown.

List of Japanese Aircraft used by the AdA in Indochina, 1945–1947[7]				
Type	**Unit**	**Registration**	**Entry into service**	**End of service**
A6M2 'Zero'			Dec. 1945	
Ki-21 'Sally'			Feb. 1946	
Ki-30 'Ann'	GT I/34		Jan./Feb. 1946	4 Apr. 1946 (destroyed)
Ki-46 I 'Dinah'	GC II/7		27 Feb. 1946	1 Apr. 1946
Ki-46 II 'Dinah'	GC II/7		27 Feb. 1946	1 Apr. 1946
Ki-46 II 'Dinah'	GC II/7		27 Feb. 1946	1 Apr. 1946
Ki-46 III 'Dinah'	GC II/7		27 Feb. 1946	12 June 1946 (destroyed)
Ki-51 'Sonia'	SAL 99		Feb. 1946	18 July 1946
Ki-51 'Sonia'	SAL 99		Feb. 1946	18 July 1946
Ki-34 'Thora'	SAL 99		Jan./Feb. 1946	10 Jan. 1946 (destroyed)
Ki-43 III 'Oscar'	GC II/7		9 Dec. 1945	20 Dec. 1945 (destroyed)
Ki-43 'Oscar'	GC I/7	6083	Dec. 1945	7 Feb. 1946 (destroyed)
Ki-43 III 'Oscar'	GC I/7	7007	Dec. 1945	13 Dec. 1945 (destroyed)
Ki-43 'Oscar'	GC I/7	7076	Dec. 1945	12 Dec. 1945 (destroyed)
Ki-43 III 'Oscar'	GC II/7	7188	9 Dec. 1945	7 Feb. 1946
Ki-43 III 'Oscar'	GC I/7	7467	Dec. 1945	7 Feb. 1946
Ki-43 III 'Oscar'	GC I/7	7620	Dec. 1945	7 Jan. 1946 (destroyed)
Ki-43 III 'Oscar'	GC I/7	7690	Dec. 1945	25 Jan. 1946 (destroyed)
Ki-43 'Oscar'	GC I/7	7698	Dec. 1945	2 Jan. 1946 (destroyed)
Ki-43 III 'Oscar'	GC I/7	7713	Dec. 1945	26 Jan. 1946 (destroyed)
Ki-43 III 'Oscar'	GC I/7	7715	Dec. 1945	7 Feb. 1946
Ki-43 III 'Oscar'	GC I/7	7764	Dec. 1945	18 Dec. 1945 (destroyed)
Ki-43 III 'Oscar'	GC II/7	7790	9 Dec. 1945	30 July 1946 (destroyed)
L2D3 'Tabby'	GT I/34	7826	Feb. 1946	Feb. 1946
Ki-36 'Ida'	SAL 99	7952	Feb. 1946	23 Apr. 1946
Ki-36 'Ida'	SAL 99	4265	Feb. 1946	3 Mar. 1946 (destroyed)
Ki-36 'Ida'	SAL 99	10580	Feb. 1946	5 Apr. 1946 (destroyed)
Ki-36 'Ida'	SAL 99		Feb. 1946	Mar. 1946
Ki-36 'Ida'	SAL 99		18 Feb. 1946	20 June 1946
Ki-36 'Ida'	SAL 99		Mar. 1946	20 May 1947
Ki-54 'Hickory'	SAL 99		Feb. 1946	21 Nov. 1946
Ki-54 'Hickory'	SAL 99		Feb. 1946	28 Feb. 1947
Ki-54 'Hickory'	SAL 99		Feb. 1946	20 May 1947
Ki-54 'Hickory'	SAL 99		Feb. 1946	18 July 1947
Ki-54 'Hickory'	SAL 99		Feb. 1946	20 May 1947
Ki-54 'Hickory'	SAL 99		Feb. 1946	May 1947
Ki-54 'Hickory'			Feb. 1946	

The de Havilland DH.98 Mosquito FB.Mk 6 was a British twin-engined, shoulder-winged and multi-role aircraft that made its first operational flight on 15 November 1941. Though it served a number of Allies well during the Second World War, its wooden frame was not adapted to the humidity presented by the Indochinese landscape. (Author's collection)

The Reorganisation of France's Airforce Operations in Indochina

French aviation in Indochina played a highly important role in taking back and keeping areas captured by the Viet Minh in 1945 and 1946. By May 1947, the AdA's fighter groups had flown around 8,000 hours and over 5,000 missions. As the conflict intensified and widened in 1947, to improve the coordination of aerial forces the new head of the AdA, General de Brigade Aérienne Pierre Bodet, divided up the Indochinese air space into two sectors known as *Groupements Tactiques*, or 'Tactical Groups'. One headquartered in Bach Mai, Hanoi covered the northern Indochina operational zone while responsibility for operations in the southern zone fell to the HQ at Tan Son Nhut,

Saigon. A third 'Tactical Group' based at Hué and Nha Trang was created in 1948 to handle operations in central Indochina. In March 1950, Bodet was replaced by General André Hartemann who proceeded to create *Groupements Aériens Tactictiques* (GATACs), or 'Aerial Tactical Groups'. Covering the same areas as their predecessors, the new formations were intended to allow for greater coordination and cooperation between the different branches of French armed forces in Indochina. This was overseen by an inter-branch organisation known as the *Etat-Major Inter-Armes des Forces Terrestres* (EMIFT).

The 4e *Escadre de Chasse* (September 1947 to January 1949)

Composition : GC I/4 'Dauphiné' and GC II/4 'La Fayette'.

Based in Koblenz, Germany the 4 EC left France aboard the French vessel *Felix Roussel* on 16 August 1947 and arrived in Saigon on 14 September. A replacement for 2 EC, GC I/4 set up operations in Nha Trang while 2/4 replaced GC I/2 at Gia Lam. Still using Spitfires, GC II/4 carries out its first mission on 22 September 1947 when it gives air support to a French outpost surrounded by the VM.

As for GC I/4, its first mission was on 18 September when machine gunning VM positions. In October, the fighter group was split up into smaller units and operated out of Tan Son Nhut, Tourane, and Dong Hoi. Although the group's main role was to provide air support for ground and amphibious operations, the scope of these operations was limited by the monsoon season which takes place in southwestern Indochina from April to September each year. Nonetheless, up to its departure from Indochina on 31 August 1948, the 4e EC carried out over 7,500 sorties.

The 3e EC (September 1948 to April 1950) and the 5e EC (July 1949–1951)

Composition 3e EC: GC I/3 'Navarre' and GC II/3 'Champagne'. Sub-units 'Navarre', SPA 95 and SPA 153; sub-units 'Champagne', SPA 67 and SPA 75.

Composition 5e EC: GC I/5 'Vendée' and GC II/5 'Ile-

de-France'. Sub-units 'Vendée', SPA 26 and SPA 124; 'Groupe Ile-de-France'.

Based in Friedrichshafen, Germany, the 3e EC replaced the 4e EC on 24 September 1948 when GC I/3 arrived at Haiphong and made its way to the Base Aérienne 197 (BA 197) at Gia Lam. As for GC II/3, before arriving in Indochina, it made its way to Oran, Algeria

France received its first Bell P-63 Kingcobras near the end of the Second World War and would use around 60 examples of this fighter until 1950. This photo shows some of the Kingcobras of Normandie-Niemen on the runway at Tan Son Nhut. (Author's collection)

Pictured here in Algeria, the NC.701 Martinet was a German-designed, but French-built trainer adapted for aerial reconnaissance by the French Air Force. Crewed by two personnel but able to carry eight passengers, the NC.701 was powered by two Renault 12S-00 V-12 inverted air-cooled piston engines each generating 590 hp. (Author's collection)

where its pilots familiarised themselves with Spitfires. Until then, both fighter groups had operated the Republic P-47 Thunderbolt.

On arrival, SPA 75 was subsequently based at Tourane while SPA 67 was based at Tan Son Nhut. On 26 September, the squadron took charge of the first 12 of its Spitfires while waiting for replacements. When these replacements did arrive, it was found however, that certain parts had been sabotaged by communist sympathisers in the workshops where the different parts of Spitfires were assembled after shipment from Great Britain. These sympathisers supported the VM rather than their own forces and it was discovered that the replacements' head gaskets had been damaged or that iron filings had been placed in the oil pumps of the aircraft' engines.

In spite of other drawbacks such as the typhoons present in southern Indochina towards the end of the year, the aircraft of the 3e EC carried out their first sorties on 31 December 1948. As with the AdA's other fighter units, its missions included strafing enemy positions, attacking vessels suspected of transporting men and arms and acting as cover for transport aircraft carrying paratroopers.

Though remaining in Indochina until April 1950, in January 1949 the 3e EC was joined by the 5e EC, a moment that saw the gradual introduction of the Bell P-63 Kingcobra. The introduction of this US-manufactured fighter into the Indochinese theatre came about after several examples were transferred from El Aouina in Tunisia to Marignane near Marseilles on 13 June 1949. Here, the aircraft were disassembled and packaged before being shipped to Saigon aboard the aircraft carrier *Dixmude*.

The Kingcobras arrived in Indochina on 22 July 1949 and the first test flights were carried out on 10 August. The aircraft became operational on 31 August 1949 when GC I/5 took part in the aptly named Operation *Cobra* in and around the Plain of Reeds and GC II/5 flew operations along the Mekong River. More operations involving the Cobras took place in September 1949 when, along

AAC.1 Toucans were converted for service as bombers. Here, examples of the aircraft line up at Bien Hoa in July 1946. The AAC.1 Toucan was a copy of the German-designed Junkers Ju52/3m produced mainly at Amiot's workshops in Colombes, France for use by the Luftwaffe from 1944. After the war, over 200 models were transferred to the French Air Force. (Author's collection)

The Showa L2D3 'Tabby' performed a similar function to the AAC.1 Toucan and its development was based on the Douglas DC-3. The examples used by the French in Indochina were the Type 0 Transport Model 22 powered by a Mitsubishi Kinsei 51, 52 or 53 engines each generating 1,300 hp. The French gave the AAC.1 the nickname 'Tante Julie', or 'Aunt Julie'. (Author's collection)

with six Spitfires, eight of the American aircraft cleared areas around the *Route Coloniale* 4.[8]

The GC II/6 'Normandie-Niemen' (October 1949–1951)

One of France's most celebrated fighter squadrons, on 20 June 1949, the AdA's general staff announced that the GC II/6 would be trading in its Mosquito fighter-bombers and would now be flying Spitfires in Indochina. However, due France's fleet of this fighter plane becoming fatigued by the humidity found in the Far East, this exchange did not materialise. Instead, just a few weeks later, the group's pilots were training on Kingcobras in the Tunisian desert around France's Bizerte-Sidi Ahmed airbase in Tunisia.

By the end of September 1949, the crews of Normandie-Niemen were putting the finishing touches to their flying techniques on this aircraft and on 6 October, they left Tunisia bound for Saigon. GC II/6 made its first flight on Kingcobras on 13 November and two weeks later, it made its first attack in the Cao Lang sector when sinking a number of sampans.[9] More operations will be discussed in volume 2 of this series.

Escadrille de Reconnaissance d'Outre-Mer (EROM 80) – September 1949

Although the group known as EROM 80 was not, strictly speaking, a fighter squadron, it finds it inclusion in this section due to its operating US-supplied Grumman F8F Bearcats from May 1951. The group was created in early 1949 after concerns were raised over the failings of intelligence provided by aerial observation units (see after). What the AdA needed, and what the EROM was to provide, was reconnaissance backed up by photographic evidence.

The squadron was formed using specialists from the 33rd Reconnaissance Squadron (33e *Escadre de Reconnaissance*) based at Boufarik, Algeria. In June 1949, three NC.701 Martinets were shipped to Saigon while the unit's personnel arrived on 23 August. As it was discovered that the Martinets had, again, been damaged by pro-communist dockers in France, training for the EROM's mission was carried out on the Morane-Saulnier MS-500 Criquet, or on Spitfire 9s and P-63s that had already been adapted for photo reconnaissance.

The unit's first operational base was Tan Son Nhut, but as its airstrip tended to become boggy and difficult to use, so operations were transferred to Bien Hoa. By November 1949, the unit was using six Martinets and on 12 November, it carried out its first mapping mission over Bien Hoa and the Plain of Reeds. Given the context that was developing (see later), the unit's most important mission up to 1950 was undoubtedly that carried out on 22 November 1949 after a detachment was sent to Gia Lam. From here, the EROM 80 carried out extensive operations in order to document VM supply lines above the border separating China and Tonkin.[10]

Transport/Bomber Groups

Composition: *Escadrille de Marche en Extrême-Orient* (EMEO) that became the *Groupe de Marche d'Extrême-Orient* (GMEO) or *Groupe de Marche de Transport en Extrême-Orient* (GMTEO) in November 1945.

The EMEO was formed using detachments from the GT I/15 'Touraine' based at Valence, and the GT II/15 'Anjou' based at Lyon-Bron. The two groups assembled in Damascus, Syria before leaving for Jessore, India on 9 September where they joined the RAF's 357 Squadron. As soon as Tan Son Nhut airfield was opened at the end of the month, one detachment of the EMEO used it as its base and operated Douglas C-47s, while the remainder of the EMEO stayed in Jessore.

In October and November 1945, the Jessore detachments took part in operations Kay 1 and Kay 2. These were Franco-British operations led by Force 136 of the Special Air Service and the French *Service d'Action* intended to give support to Franco-Laotian forces battling the Viet Minh. From November 1945, all detachments of the now GMTEO, were based at Tan Son Nhut where they operated 18 C-47s. The group's missions included the transport of crews from EC I/17 to Phnom Penh in early December 1945 and a similar operation on 23 January 1946 when taking troops to Dalat in southern Annam.

In February 1946, the transport group brought in supplies and ammunition to the 9th DIC which was making its way from the Mekong Valley to Paksé. The GMTEO operated 23 C-47s at the time, but the arrival of the *Groupe de Transport* GT I/34 'Béarn' on 10 February 1946, signalled the entrance of the AAC.1 Toucan into service. Some sources indicate that the GT I/34 also flew a number of Mitsubishi Ki-21 'Sallys', and Showa L2D3 'Tabbys'.

Groupe de Transport: GT II/15 'Anjou', then GT II/64 (from July 1946)

Created in 1940, at the end of the Second World War GT II/15 operated C-47s from Lyon-Bron before transferring to Valence. Three C-47s from GT II/15 were used to make up the fleet used by the EMEO and in July 1946, the remainder of the group arrived at Tan Son Nhut. From mid-December, the group flew in support of troops under attack from the VM in Tonkin and central Anna, and its aircraft participated in operations in Laos and along the Mekong Valley. The latter consisted of dropping supplies and weapons over isolated outposts situated high in the mountains. On 1 July 1947, GT II/15 became GT II/64. It continued to transport supplies and took part in bombing missions when required.

GT I/34, then 1/64 'Béarn' (from February 1946)

Previously operating the Douglas DB-7, in early 1945 GT I/34 began a switchover to the Martin B-26 Marauder at its base in Djedeida, Tunisia. However, in November 1945 it, too, was designated to use the AAC.1 Toucan and the Douglas C-47. Leaving Marseilles in January 1946, the group arrived in Indochina on 7 February where it was based at Bien Hoa.

As well as its allocation of French-supplied aircraft, GT I/34 also recuperated Mitsubishi Ki-21s, Tachikawa Ki-54s, Ki-46s, and Showa L2D3s left by the Japanese. In February 1947, GT I/34 left

Bien Hoa for Tan Son Nhut having already completed nearly 5,000 missions and 10,000 flying hours.[11] It became 1/64 in July 1947, and in October of that year the group took part in Operation Léa after sending a 12-aircraft detachment to Bach Mai near Hanoi. The group returned to Tan Son Nhut in December 1947 and throughout 1948 and 1949, it participated in pacification operations in Cochinchina, Annam and Cambodia. Notably, the group provided air support for ground movements during the build up to the Battle of Route Coloniale 4 (early 1950). As the VM increased the number of ambushes it carried out along the RC4 in 1949, GT I/64 helped evacuate civilian populations in Cao Bang, That Khé, Dong Dang and Lang Son as well as assuming the type of bombing missions mentioned previously.

GT III/64 'Tonkin' (November 1947 – July 1948)

A plan to bring more troops into Tonkin and Laos in late 1947 resulted in the creation of a supplementary transport group operating AAC.1 Toucans. Formed using personnel of the GT IV/15 based at Chartres in October 1947, the air and ground crews of GT III/64 were stationed at Bach Mai from 4 December that year. The first operation took place two days later and consisted of dropping supplies over Lang Hit. Similar missions followed until July 1948 during which time GT III/64 transported paratroopers in operations in Tonkin and northern Laos. The departure of GT III/64 meant that 1/64 'Béarn' was the sole French transport group left in Indochina until the arrival of GT II/62 'Franche-Comté' in August 1949.[12]

GT II/62 'Franche-Comté' (from August 1949)

At the end of the Second World War, the then bomber group 2/52 was based at Bilda, Algeria. Becoming a transport group in November 1946 and redesignated GT II/52, the group formed part of the 62nd Transport Squadron (62e Escadre de transport) and operated B-26 Marauders as well as AAC.1 Toucans. After being designated for transfer to Indochina, it maintained the use of the AAC.1s and was stationed at Bach Mai. The group carried out its first mission on 3 October 1949.

Liaison Aircraft

The *Section d'Avions de Liaison* 99 (SAL) based at Bien Hoa, then Tan Son Nhut, operated four Mitsubishi Ki-46 'Dinah', seven Tachikawa Ki-54 'Hickory', two Mitsubishi Ki-51 'Sonia', and four Tachikawa Ki-36 'Ida' left by the Japanese.[13] France also obtained a Mitsubishi Ki-30 'Ann'. It started life as a light tactical bomber in the service of the IJA, but the French used it as a daylight visual patrol aircraft.

The MS.500 Criquet was the French designation for the German-made Fieseler Fi 156 Storch. Another aircraft resulting from the requirement for French manufacturers to produce war materials for Nazi Germany during the occupation of France, the Criquet was used extensively in Indochina as it was able to take off from strips as short as 60 metres (196 ft.) with a landing distance of some 20 metres (65 ft.). This meant that the Criquet could perform many of the duties that were out of reach for larger aircraft such as the DC-3. (Author's collection)

Until it was scrapped in 1946, its duties also included ferrying French pilots to other airbases in Indochina. Lastly, France converted two Ki-51 'Sonias' from dive bombers to liaison aircraft. The aircraft's bomb racks and rearwards-facing machine guns were removed, and the aircraft were assigned to the SAL 99. Of all the Japanese aircraft used, only the Ki-54 was deemed satisfactory for use by French crews, and from April 1946, the unit received three Morane-Saulnier MS.500s, and three Stinson L-5s. Before the SAL 99 became the Aerial Liaison Squadron 52 (*Escadrille de Liaisons Aériennes* 52) in April 1948, its inventory was completed by Nord Pingouin 1000s, and two German-made Bücker Bü 181s previously used by the 1e EC. Finally, two Siebel S1 204s were used from the beginning of 1948 for longer trips. Though based in Saigon, the SAL 99/ELA 52 was used in missions throughout Cochinchina due to its adaptability to a range of duties including the delivery of letters, medical supplies, medevac and provided the type of liaisons to which larger aircraft were not suited.

Two developments in April 1948 greatly improved France's capacity to seek out and destroy enemy bases as the VM retreated to the Indochinese and Chinese hinterlands to prepare the next phase of its strategy. Firstly, April 1948 saw the creation of the ELA 53 based at Bach Mai, and six months later ELA 52 received its first NC.701s. Now, not only could the ELAs carry out photo reconnaissance missions, but they could attack enemy positions if they were detected. The Martinets were armed with four machine guns in the nose of the aircraft and a MAC 34 could be set up in a port-side hatch to provide extra fire power. Many of the medevac and light transport duties performed by the ELA's variety of aircraft were transferred to the Hilier 360 helicopter in early 1950, a section that will be dealt with in the second volume in this series.

In a similar fashion to the French Air Force, French naval aviation was to take advantage of the aircraft left by Japanese forces in Indochina. This was the case for this Nakajima A6M2-N 'Rufe' which is pictured wearing the markings of the Allied Technical Air Intelligence Unit. This example is possibly the formerly registered BI-12 of the IJA's 381 kokutai, and what is known is that it was used by Escadrille 8F at Bien Hoa after undergoing testing by the ATAUI in Singapore from March 1946. It was destroyed in a crash near Rach Ba sang on 19 September of that year. (Author's collection)

The Consolidated Model 28, or PBY Catalina in US Navy service, was a flying boat and amphibious aircraft that entered service in October 1936. The Catalina could be used for duties such as anti-submarine warfare, but in Indochina it served a variety of purposes such as the transporting of troops and supplies. (Author's collection)

Another Japanese aircraft taken over by French naval aviation was this Aichi E3A 'Jake' pictured aboard a French aircraft carrier in Ha Long Bay in January 1946 (Author's collection)

Other 'Jakes' were put into service as medivac aircraft (Author's collection)

Army Aviation

Pelton d'Avions d'Artillerie (PAA)/*Peleton d'Avions* 9e DIC (PA)
November 1945 – May 1947

The PAA was a group created for use by the *Aviation légère d'obsevartion d'artillerie* (ALOA) and was one of the first units to arrive in Indochina. It arrived at the same time (November 1945) as the 2e DB and the 9e DIC artillery and infantry divisions. The purpose of the unit was to spot enemy artillery and/or to guide

General Pierre Boyer de Latour pictured in 1946. As well as taking part in fighting in Tunisia in 1942, the then Colonel Boyer de Latour's 4e *Régiment de Ttirailleurs Marocains* saw action in Corsica and were part of French forces that helped liberate southern France in 1944. Promoted to the rank of general in 1946, Boyer de Latour was also appointed commissioner of Cochinchina. (public domain)

Ground crew handling an unidentified Spitfire (probably of the GC.II/4), into its parking position. (Albert Grandolini Collection)

A front view at a fully bombed-up Spitfire, shortly before take off. (Albert Grandolini Collection)

A pair of worn-out Spirfire LF.Mk IXs – both armed with 30kg bombs in addition to cannons and machine guns – underway for a mission over western Tonkin. (Albert Grandolini Collection)

A C-47 (probably of the GMTEO) in worn out dark olive drab overall camouflage as seen while loading supplies. (Albert Grandolini Collection)

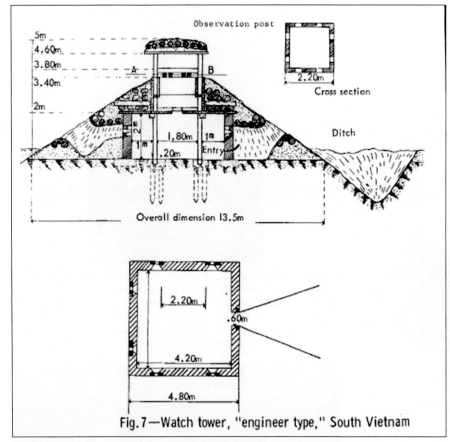

Fig. 7—Watch tower, "engineer type," South Vietnam

The first watch towers were fairly rudimentary structures housing up to six men. Placed around 600 yards from each other, while the watch tower system worked reasonably well in the flatlands of Cochinchina, visibility was reduced in Tonkin due to its hilly terrain and jungles. This photo shows how bamboo was used to provide protection from attack. (Author's collection)

1er *Groupe d'Aviation d'Observation d'Artillerie* (1er GAOA).

The 1er GAOA left France aboard the French vessel MS *Boissevin* on 18 December 1945 and arrived at Cap St. Jacques (now Vung Tau) before heading northwards by boat to Ha Long Bay and setting up base at Cat Bi in March 1946. The group received its first MS.500s shortly after and it wasted no time in becoming operational as VM activity in Tonkin increased in intensity. From May 1946, one section (1e Esc.) of the GAOA was based at Tourane (Da Nang) operating four MS.500s, while another (2e Esc.) operated four MS.500s from Seno airfield near Savannakhet, Laos. In July 1946, the 2e Esc. left for Tourane and the 1e Esc. was sent to Tonkin as the shape of the war changed. The group was disbanded in September 1950 to form the 21e GAOA.[14]

2e *Groupe d'Aviation d'Observation d'Artillerie* (2e GAOA)

Attached to the 3e DIC, the 2e GAOA arrived in Saigon on 10 March 1946. First operating the Piper L-4H and the Stinson L-5, the group then switched to MS.500s. Its first mission took place on 27 April 1946 in the Phu Loi region just north of Saigon and a year later, it was still operating from Tan Son Nhut where it was responsible for covering movements around Annam. The group disbanded at the same time as the 1e GAOA and became the 22e GAOA.

artillery fire and its aircraft consisted of the Piper L-4H Grasshopper and the Stinson L-5 Sentinel.

The PAA was first deployed during operations in Cochinchina from 2 December 1945, then in clearing operations around Ban Me Thuot and Nha Trang between 25 January and 15 February 1946. Both the L-4H and the L-5 were used extensively for duties including medivac and carrying supplies to isolated outposts. The PAA was disbanded in August 1946 to form the PA 9e DIC and in turn, the PA 9e DIC was disbanded in May 1947 and was integrated into the 3e *Groupe Aérien d'Obsevation d'Artillerie* (GAOA).

Naval Aviation

Flottille 8F

A reorganisation of French naval aviation in September 1945 led to the creation of the *Forces Navales d'Extrême-Orient* (FNEO). As was the case for the France's riverine forces in Indochina, these 'Far East naval forces' were commanded by Admiral Henri Nomy (himself a former naval pilot) and they were divided up into three main bodies: a general staff; the *Flottille* 8FE ('fleet'); and a mobile group transferable between naval units.

While the FNEO received its orders to deploy to Indochina, the four PBY Catalinas it had been designated to use in upcoming operations were based at Agadir, Morocco. Leaving Agadir for Le Bourget airport on 4 October 1945, after a journey with stops in Malta, Egypt, Bahrain and India, the aircraft (serial nos. 46566, 567, 570 and 574) finally arrived in Saigon on 29 October. Based at Tan Son Nhut, the Catalinas carried out their first missions from 1 November. Although

The fortifications were placed at strategic points along roads and rivers. Here, riverine forces pull up alongside a watch tower in the Mekong Delta. (Author's collection)

these missions consisted mainly of reconnoitring the surrounding areas, as the air force's Spitfires were just in the process of becoming operational, the Catalinas were used to provide air cover for ground troops. The Catalinas also served as troop carriers due to their being able to operate over long distances. It is not surprising that their pilots found themselves flying inland to destinations as far from

the coast as Laos or the Central Plateaux. By December 1946, more Catalinas had been deployed to Siem Reap in Cambodia and they were to take part in operations on 19 December when dropping French paratroopers over Hanoi. Other interventions included Operation *Pierre* from 1–7 February 1948.

6
THE EVER-CHANGING FACE OF THE FIRST INDOCHINA WAR, 1948 – 1949

If 1947 ended on a good note with both Laos and Cambodia joining the French Union on 23 December, the truth of the matter was that French forces were struggling to contain an elusive enemy that had been driven into its bases in Vietnam's hinterlands rather than having been destroyed. Despite the problem for French forces being one of not being able to encounter the Viet Minh in any large-scale battle up to that point (end of 1947), French commanders considered it essential to maintain the cohesiveness of their dispositions which, as we have seen, consisted of separated areas of command each attempting to pacify and keep control of different sectors. Preventing

the VM from enacting its plans was naturally to come through a series of operations that continued throughout 1948–1949, however, what the CEFEO needed was to put in place a more permanent option that would see a continuous military presence in the rural areas favoured by the Viet Minh for the carrying out of attacks and the spreading of propaganda.

Tactical Developments

Discussions about how a more ubiquitous presence could be achieved began with the arrival of General Pierre Boyer de Latour du Moulin as the commander of the *Troupes Françaises Indochine Sud* (TFIS) in July 1947. A highly decorated veteran of both world wars and the former commander of a battalion of *Tirailleurs Marocains* and now head of military and civil operations in Cochinchina, Boyer de Latour's knowledge and experience of conflict in the deserts of North Africa led to the establishment of an extensive system of fortified military bunkers throughout the province that were capable of resisting armed assaults and thus deterring the enemy from carrying out further attacks.

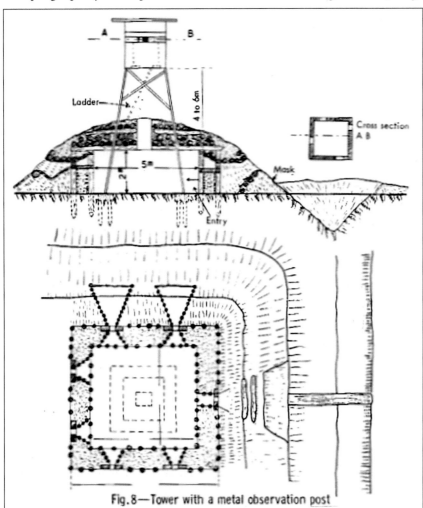

Fig. 8—Tower with a metal observation post

Later, the watch tower system was developed so that blockhouses and compounds, such as the one pictured, formed a defensive line. Artillery could be placed inside the perimeters to ward off attacks by the Viet Minh. (Author's collection)

French forces were able to use the forts as a base from which they could start foot patrols with another consideration being that if forts were placed at strategic points such as near villages or along important lines of access into rural areas, then the French could cut off the Viet Minh from its most significant source of recruitment – the Vietnamese population itself.

Though it is valuable to an understanding of French strategy and tactics used in the Indochina War – tactics that were also applied in Tonkin and Annam – taking a closer look at the bunker system is equally valuable as it provides an insight into daily life for most French combat forces in Indochina during this period and the ones following: the manning of watch towers in far-flung rural zones to keep the Viet Minh at bay.

The Fortification System

As noted, the main purpose of the fortifications was to defend a given area (a village or a larger area) from attack by guerrillas. The reason behind this was to protect local populations, to create

Portrait of a soldier of the 13e *Demi-brigade de Légion Etrangère*: Zygmunt Jatczak

Born in Warsaw in 1924, at 15 years old Jatczak witnessed the bombing and the occupation of the city by Nazi Germany that resulted in the deaths of nearly 40,000 civilians. In January 1943, Jatczak was sent to Majdanek concentration camp on the outskirts of Lublin, Poland and it was here he saw thousands sent to the camp's seven gas chambers. He managed to escape from the camp shortly after his internment and in March 1943, he joined the Miotla Battalion of the Polish resistance. Like many of the other thousands of Polish men and women, Jatczak took part in the Warsaw Uprising that began on 1 August 1944.

Although captured and imprisoned at Stalag X-B (Sandbostel) and camp Westertimke (Bremen) by the Nazis, at the end of April 1945 he was liberated by the British Army. In 1947, Jatczak decided that he wanted to join the Foreign Legion and travelled to Strasbourg to do so. He spent two months at Sidi Bel Abbes before being sent to Indochina and here, Jatczak joined the 3rd Company of the 1st Battalion of the 13e DBLE stationed at Ca Mau in Cochinchina. He took part in fighting around the Ca Mau area, as well as around Cu Chi, but after being wounded in action, he returned to France in 1962.

Zygmunt Jatczak was a member of the Polish resistance before joining the French Foreign Legion. He served in Indochina where, ironically, former members of the SS and the Wehrmacht were among those who made up the ranks of France's foreign contingent in the war. (Author's collection)

an ideological distance between them and the Viet Minh and to reinforce the notion that France was the only legitimate authority.

Compared to later versions, the watch towers set up in 1948 were fairly rudimentary and consisted most commonly of four brick walls topped by roofing slates. The walls were between 25 to 40cm thick (8 to 15in) and were supplemented by a low wall that surrounded the building. The entrance to the fortification was located at least two metres (6.5 ft) above ground level and the observation post was to be found at a height of five to six metres (15–20 ft) with an overhang to allow the throwing of grenades.

For earlier versions, a ladder on the outside of the building gave access to the entrance, but later versions were fitted with internal ladders giving more protection. The thickness of the walls for versions built from 1949 was also increased and fortifications often contained inner and outer walls made of reinforced concrete, tree trunks, or bamboo fences. This was an important consideration as guerrillas would often place explosives at the base of the fort in an attempt to weaken its structure. The explosives could be placed either by hand or by attaching them to long poles made of bamboo.[1]

The forts – one kilometre apart (600 yards) from each other – were usually manned by four to six men, but larger observation posts, named '*tours-mères*' or 'mother towers', contained larger numbers of men and were armed accordingly. As for this weaponry, the men were equipped with a variety of pistols, rifles, machine guns and other ordnance including the Hotchkiss M1922 machine guns, or the MAS-36 bolt-action rifle, a weapon used extensively by French forces in Indochina.

Life for soldiers posted to a watch tower was repetitive and monotonous. At first light, a patrol was sent out to search the surroundings for booby traps potentially set up overnight by local guerrillas. The days were spent either reinforcing the watch tower's defences, cleaning weapons and maintaining physical fitness through playing sports such as volleyball. For entertainment, card games would be organised and occasionally, the soldiers would go to a nearby village to drink a homemade, traditional rice wine

known as '*ruou de*'. Sometimes, soldiers tended vegetable gardens set up outside.

Letter writing was also an important activity. Written correspondence with wives, girlfriends or families enabled soldiers in Indochina to keep abreast of events back home or to reassure loved ones. As this activity greatly contributed to keeping up morale, six aircraft ensured that mail was sent and delivered three times per week. However, it could take up to three weeks to reach its destination as soldiers were moved to different units or different places.

At night, a watch tower's inhabitants would listen out for the slightest noise that could alert those on night watch to the presence of an enemy attempting to launch a surprise attack. Tin cans were placed on barbed wire in the inner-perimeter of the compound to help detect enemy movement, though often any alarm was set off by rats, birds, or even the wind. If there was to be an attack, it usually occurred during the six-hour period between the setting and the rising of the sun according to the different seasons and the position of the moon.

Attacks could be sudden. Several hundred assailants could throw themselves at the barbed wire or bamboo fences to create a gap, then successive waves of Viet Minh would attempt to overrun the watch tower or compound. The attacks could last for several hours and if the defence of a position had been successful then air support could be called in to clear the area either through bombing raids or by machine gunning Viet Minh positions.

The morning after was spent making sure that booby traps or mines had not been placed around the camp. If men had been killed or wounded, they had to be evacuated; if a watch tower's ammunition had been used up, it had to be replaced. An attack could serve as a pretext for the setting up of the ambush of those carrying out this work so extreme vigilance was necessary in areas of intense Viet Minh activity.

Although watch towers in Cochinchina and Annam were less likely to be the target of such an attack, Tonkin presented a different context due to the numbers of Viet Minh active in the province. As

Portrait of a Viet Minh commander: Huynh Van Nge

Born into a peasant family on 2 February 1914 in the village of Tan Tich (Chanh My Ha canton, Bien Hoa province), Huynh Van Nghe led a nomadic early life on a small-holding as his family navigated the length of the Bao Luong River in search of work. A storm put an end to that existence and shortly afterwards, the family settled in Tan Uyen some 40kms (25 miles) north of Saigon.

Although the family was poor, Van Nghe managed to finish primary schooling in 1928 and after obtaining a scholarship, the future VM commander attended the Lycée Petrus Ky in Saigon, a high school set up by the French to provide an opportunity to gifted Vietnamese children. This did not stop the young Huynh Van Nge resenting colonialism and it was in Saigon that he discovered communism to be a means of expressing this resentment.

On leaving high school in 1932, he found work with Indochina Railways and in 1936, he joined the Indochinese Congress, a people's assembly in which the Vietnamese could negotiate colonial reforms with the French. At this time, Van Nghe also began to write and publish poetry and newspaper articles using the pseudonym, Hoang Ho. In 1937, his association with the Congress led him to join the Indochinese Communist Party.

Forced to seek refuge in Thailand after the Cochinchina uprising of 1940, from here Van Nghe gave active support to Vietnamese movements calling for an end to French rule. On his return to Vietnam in 1944, he contacted Tran Van Giau – the Secretary of the Cochinchina Party Committee and the Chairman of the Southern Resistance Committee – and through this contact, Van Nghe was given the job of establishing anti-French revolutionary activity in Bien Hoa.

In July 1945 after joining the ICP, Van Nghe took part in the Viet Minh's uprising in Cochinchina and was assigned to command the Bien Hoa Liberation Army and to advise the VM's Eastern Resistance Committee. After French forces reoccupied Bien Hoa and Thu Dat Mot in October 1945, Van Nghe set up a base at Tan Uyen where he organised the provision of supplies and food to soldiers of the VM's Zone VII commanded by Nguyen Binh. Before long, Tan Uyen became one of the strongest VM bases in the south and in April 1946, Van Nghe was appointed military commissioner of the Bien Hoa province. This role required Van Nge to coordinate the activities of two armed groups active in the area around Bien Hoa: the Chau Thanh, the Long Thanh and Bien Hoa national guards.

In May 1946, a military conference was held in the VM's 'War Zone D' (see Part Three) and here it was decided to unify all the different armed groups active in the Bien Hoa province. This merger led to the creation of the 10th *Chi Doi*. Van Nge was appointed as commander of the battalion, Nguyen Van Lung acted as his second in command and Phan Dinh Cong took care of political affairs.

The 10th *Chi Doi* was made up of 2,000 soldiers organised into three companies

Huynh Van Nge was the commander of the Viet Minh's 10th *Chi Doi*. (Author's collection)

designated A, B and C. In turn, A company was divided into three platoons (1, 2, and 3) commanded by Vo Tinh Quan and operating in the Tan Uyen area; company B consisted of 4, 5, and six platoons were commanded by Le Van Ngoc and operated in the Xuan Loc and Chau Thanh areas, whilst the last two platoons (7 and 8), were commanded by Luong Van Nho and operated around Long Thanh.

Whilst March 1948 saw Van Nge lead the attack on the Dalat convoy, in July 1948 he took over command of Zone VII. He developed tactics whereby the VM could successfully attack and destroy watch towers and his tactics proved to be so popular that they were adopted by other VM units active in Indochina. Although Van Nghe put a temporary end to his military career after serving as the VM's Deputy Director of Military Training in Hanoi, in 1965 he returned to the south to help the Viet Cong. Van Nghe died in Saigon (then Ho Chi Minh City) in March 1977.[9]

Members of the mixed French-Viet Minh Military Commission, as seen in early 1946, in front of one the AAC.1s (French-manufactured Junkers Ju-52 transport). (Albert Grandolini Collection)

it was therefore nearly impossible to stop every attack, the French developed and implemented early warning systems that gave watch towers and compounds time to prepare. In this case, a group of two or three, well-armed men equipped with walkie-talkies set up a position some 500 yards away.

As the following diagrams show, by 1950 several modifications had been made to improve the resistance of the watch towers and other fortifications. French engineers had designed and built veritable blockhouses capable of housing 20 men or more, the walls of the structures became thicker and defences were strengthened so that fortifications in Indochina evoked images of the north African desert campaigns fought by Legionnaires of the past. The blockhouse building project continued well into the early 1950s under the auspices of General Jean de Lattre de Tassigny. Indeed, the so-called De Lattre Line was a series of fortifications and weapons installations built around the Red River Delta. The line consisted of around 1,200 blockhouses able to withstand Viet Minh artillery fire spread over a distance of some 235 miles (378km). They were linked by roads able to bear the weight of France's largest tanks. A drawback was this type of fortification was immobile and the Viet Minh were able to go through the gaps between compounds fairly easily, just as Nazi Germany had done by using the Ardennes forest to pierce through the Maginot Line some 10 years earlier.

Operation Véga, February 1948

The dynamics of the First Indochina War did not resemble those of the First or Second World Wars or any of France's future wars. The most important difference was that French forces combated an enemy that did not seek face-to-face confrontation as the opponent did in the aforementioned conflicts. Another variance being the conflict in Southeast Asia was far from static, immovable and merely defensive – the French went after the Viet Minh while deploying air, ground and waterborne forces, supported by increasingly efficient aircraft and means of transport.

Operations to root out the Viet Minh using these means continued. Even when Boyer de Latour oversaw the building of the first watch towers, he was in the midst of organising the largest operation in Cochinchina. Given the codename Véga, the objective of the operation was to encircle and destroy Viet Minh bases in and around the Plain of Reeds with the hope of capturing or killing the commander the Viet Minh's Zone VII, Nguyen Binh.

The outer reaches of the area was also home to Binh's training camps, his supply HQ, arms factories and eight companies of Chi Doi guerrilla fighters.[2] The commander of the operation was Lieutenant-Colonel Gabriel Brunet de Sairigné and among the 4,800 under his command, were his own men of the 13e DBLE, three Regiments of Tirailleurs Algériens, two regiments of Tirailleurs Marocains, a regiment of Tirailleurs Annamites and the 1st Regiment of the BMEO.

Two regiments of paratroopers (13th DBLE and SAS battalion) were to be dropped over the zone by the GT I/34 'Béarn', air support was given by the GC I/4 'Dauphiné' and waterborne operations were to be carried out by the Force Amphibie Sud using four squadrons of landing craft. The plan that began on 14 February 1948 was to use three pincer movements to encircle, what was suspected to be, the main base for Binh's forces.

While the role of ground troops was to saturate and sweep designated zones, that of the paratroopers and riverine forces was to seal the Viet Minh's escape routes out of the area.[3] Though some Viet Minh were encountered and around 150 killed in the coming days, the operation failed in its main goal of capturing Binh. Somehow tipped off that the French were about to launch Operation Véga, Binh had ordered his troops to leave the area on 9 February, then left the area three days later. Despite not decapitating the Viet Minh's leadership in the south, Sairigné did have some success. Large amounts of weaponry, materials used to make this weaponry plus important quantities of explosives, were captured. The French also managed to destroy Viet Minh medical facilities and over 130 junks

A Ju-52 pictured at Bach Mai, Hanoi. Operated by the GTs 1/64 and 2/62, it is being prepared to drop supplies in support of airborne troops. (Author's collection)

This photo shows how the Ju-52 was adapted from transport aircraft to bomber. (Albert Grandolini collection)

MS.500 spotters accompanying the convoy. The convoy was also guarded by around 150 soldiers armed with machine guns and rifles,[5] this guard also included Lieutenant-Colonel Sairigné, the commander of Operation *Véga*.

The convoy itself was commanded by Lieutenant Combetta of the 4e *Bataillon de dragons portés* (4e BDP) and left Saigon at 06.30. His objective was to meet up halfway with a similar convoy travelling in the opposite direction before dusk and for each of the convoys to provide mutual protection through the night. Although the line of vehicles did not encounter any major problem apart from the breakdown of a scout car in the early afternoon, around 16.00 just outside Bien Hoa, the convoy came under heavy fire laid out by some of the 500 Viet Minh from the 10th *Chi Doi* commanded by Huynh Van Nge. At that point, the convoy was spread out over a seven-kilometre long (4.3 miles) stretch of dirt road bordered by an almost vertical incline on one side and dense bush on the other. This meant that the convoy's defensive forces could not easily regroup. Lieutenant-Colonel Sairigné was killed outright in the opening burst of gunfire and in an attack that lasted two hours.

Calling in reinforcements from the nearest garrison at Bien Hoa was hampered by the surrounding, and when Saigon was finally made aware of events and dispatched Spitfires at 17.45, the actions of pilots from the GC I/4 'Dauphiné' were hindered by the cloak of the jungle and a rainstorm that had hit the area. Whereas the heavy rain did have the benefit of dousing burning vehicles with water, the damage had already been done by the time the Viet Minh left the scene around 20.30.

In what was the biggest and most successful attack mounted by the Viet Minh, according to Vietnamese sources, the 10th *Chi Doi* destroyed two companies of enemy soldiers, 63 armoured and transport vehicles and captured several French officers. For their actions, the unit was awarded the Order of Merit by the government of the DRV and Huynh Van Nge was decorated by Ho Chi Minh.[6]

Other sources provide different figures with 100 killed (including 25 French soldiers) with nearly 200 or so captured by the Viet Minh. Thirty of the captives were injured in the attack while the remainder was mostly made up of Vietnamese and Chinese traders.[7] Some 170 of those taken were subsequently freed after French forces were sent to La Nga the next day to track down the Viet Minh attackers. The forces were made up by elements of the 2e *Bataillon Coloniale de Commandos Parachutistes* (2e BCCP) of the *Garde Républicaine de Cochinchine* (GRC) and Moroccans from the 4e RTM and the 10th

and sampans used to transport rice and other foodstuffs essential for the feeding of an army.

The Battle of La Nga, 1 March 1948
The retreat of Binh's forces from their southern heartlands did not mean an end to all Viet Minh activity in Cochinchina. In fact, an event that occurred just a week or so after the end of *Vega* was to serve as another reminder that if the Viet Minh was not yet strong enough for frontal confrontation with the French Army, it did, on the other hand, possess the capacity to mount ambushes and inflict casualties on military personnel and civilians.

In July 1947, this ability to mount an ambush being one of the Viet Minh's most potent and lethal weapons, was demonstrated just when the French started to believe they were gaining the upper hand in the conflict. In this instance, a train travelling between Saigon and Phan Thiet was derailed by a mine laid on the tracks. The military escort aboard the train was quickly overcome by hundreds of partisans who set about massacring the passengers.[4] Forty people were killed.

The second example of France's susceptibility to this kind of attack came on 1 March 1948. It began when a convoy of around 70 vehicles left Saigon to travel the 186 miles (300kms) that separated the capital of Cochinchina from Dalat in Vietnam's Central Highlands. One of two weekly convoys, the route led the convoy through a section of dense tropical forest just past Bien Hoa at La Nga. This proved to be the perfect place to launch an ambush as it provided cover from the

Portrait of a Commander in the First Indochinese War: Roger Trinquier

Colonel Roger Trinquier pictured during the Algerian War. (Author's collection)

Given that the French military had relatively little experience of jungle warfare, it should be said that adaptation to the topographical conditions and the type of war being waged by the Viet Minh, took place over a short period. Some of the lessons learnt were that the Viet Minh had to be kept apart from local populations lest it indoctrinate and recruit them to its cause; some form of military presence was required to be maintained in isolated areas so as to instil the notion of legitimate authority in the minds of the aforesaid; much greater troop and equipment mobility was needed in order to confront the enemy where he was, and not where the French wanted him to be. As we have seen in the previous pages, the French learnt that increased cooperation and coordination between air, land, and sea (or riverine) forces were essential to the countering of an insurgency. In fact, the French military learnt so much about counterinsurgency from their experience in Indochina – and in the Algerian War – that two of its officers became leading authorities in the field; their theories being studied in military colleges across the world. One was David Galula who honed his methods during the latter conflict and the other was the then Commandant (Major) Roger Trinquier. Later promoted to colonel, Trinquier's relevance to this part of the volume was that not only did he develop many of the counterinsurgency methods still pertinent to today's wars, but he was also the commander of the 2e BCCP.

Roger Trinquier was born in 1908 in La Beaume, a small village situated in the Hautes-Alpes region of France. A bright student and initially destined to become a teacher, Trinquier passed the entrance examinations to a selective school in Aix-en-Provence, the *Ecole Normale*. However, as with all Frenchmen until 2001, on leaving school he had to complete two years of military service. Due to his education, Trinquier was sent to the Reserve Officer's School to teach but after taking a liking to life in the military, he requested a transfer to a French Army officer training academy to the north of Bordeaux in western France. He graduated in 1933 and was assigned to the French Marine Infantry. The regiment also known as the 'colonials', and trained specifically for overseas duty, Trinquier was soon on his way to the Far East.

As a second lieutenant, Trinquier was first sent to Lang Son, Tonkin in 1934, then he took command of an isolated French outpost at Chi-Ma on the Sino-Tonkinese border. On his return to France in 1936, Trinquier took over command of a company of the 41e *Régiment de Mitrailleurs d'Infanterie Coloniale* at Sarralbe

Chi Doi was encountered fiftykms (30 miles) from La Nga at the junction of the roads to Song Be and Dong Nai.[8] There were 40 Viet Minh killed but another 46 (mostly Vietnamese) civilians also died while others (including 10 French civilians) were never seen again.

Military Repercussions and the Increase in Airborne Operations

While the security provided to subsequent convoys was tightened, the effects of the attack on the Dalat convoy were felt both in France and among military commanders in Indochina. Although featured, paradoxically, on the front cover of *Time* magazine's edition of 1 March 1948 as the man leading Europe's charge to greater cooperation between its components with the signing of the Brussels Pact (17 March 1948), France's premier Robert Schuman came under increasing criticism of how he was handling Indochina's political situation. He ordered France's High Commissioner of Indochina, Emile Bollaert, to take immediate steps to resolve matters in Cochinchina and the commanders of operations in southern Vietnam were relieved of their duties.

In addition, repercussions were being felt regarding the fact that the Viet Minh was becoming more audacious in its actions against French forces and that these forces and their fighting material, were ill-equipped and ill-adapted to the war being waged by their opponents. Whereas Latour's fortification system partially addressed these concerns, a second initiative saw a reorganisation of the way in which airborne troops were to be used to counter the Viet Minh in areas that were out of the geographical reach of armoured regiments.

Although airborne units such as the 1/1 RCP, the 3/1 RCP and the 1er *Bataillon de Choc* were already in place and had taken part in Operation *Léa* in October 1947, the decision was made to increase their number and to put in place a specialised support group that would answer their operational requirements. Up to that point, the arrival of the *Demi-Brigade Coloniale de Commandos Parachutistes SAS* (DBSAS) in early 1946, led the creation of the *Section Technique des Unités Parachutistes* (STUP); and the arrival of the *Demi-Brigade de Marche Parachutiste* (DBMP) in Tonkin in February 1948 saw the addition of the *Section de Parachutage d'Indochine du Nord* (SPIN).

From October 1948, with the arrival of the *Groupement Léger Parachutiste* (GLP), both sections would merge to form the *Compagnie de Ravitaillement par Air des Troupes Françaises d'Indochine du Nord* (CRA/TFIN). This company was based at Bach Mai and worked alongside the GT I/64 'Béarn' and the GT II/62 'Franch-Comté' on Ju-52s and the GT II/64 'Anjou' on DC-3s. These units were to take part in Operation *Ondine* of 7-23 November 1948 (91 sorties), and Operation *Pégase* in December that year (144 sorties) dropping a total of 210 tonnes of supplies and ammunition.

Further measures to provide support to airborne troops were taken at the beginning of 1949. Led by Colonel Chavatte, the establishment of a new command structure called *Formations*

in north-eastern France. He stayed there until August 1938 when he was chosen to become a member of the marine force guarding the Concession in Shanghai. This was at a time when the Japanese had invaded China and were just about to invade French Indochina. Trinquier learnt Chinese while he was there and these language skills complemented the dialects he learnt during his time in northern Tonkin's mountains.

Promoted to the rank of captain in 1942, Trinquier never took sides in the Vichy France/Free France conflict. This decision had an effect on the length of time between his subsequent promotions as he chose to remain in the Far East, however, it did not impede him from being appointed commander of a platoon of the *Commando Ponchardier* on 3 January 1946. This unit took part in some of the earliest fighting of the war around Saigon.

On his return to France in the summer of 1946, Trinquier was first dismissed due to his non-committal to de Gaulle during the Second World War but then reinstated due to contacts he had made during his first posting in China. The officer in question was Raoul Salan, the future commander-in-chief of all French forces in Indochina and Algeria.

Following his reinstatement, in 1947 Trinquier was sent to the newly created *Ecole des Troupes Aéroportées* (ETAP or airborne troops training school) at Tarbes in southwestern France. Here, he put together another new creation, the 2e BCCP and in November 1947, Trinquier once more found himself in Indochina as a member of the TFIS.

This part of Trinquier's service saw him take part in fighting in the Plain of Reeds, and when the battalion's commander André Dupuis was killed near Saigon on 9 September 1948, Trinquier took his place and was promoted to the rank of *commandant*. On 15 November 1948, the 2e BCCP became the 2nd Battalion of the 1st Half-Brigade of Parachutists SAS (1ère *Demi-Brigade de Parachutistes SAS*: 1ère DBSAS).

Trinquier had gathered enough experience to realise that the measures put in place to counter the Viet Minh were not entirely satisfactory. In response, he approached Boyer de Latour and asked that he be given permission to try a new method of pacifying Annam by occupying a certain area, laying traps and mounting nightly ambushes to destroy the Viet Minh at a time of the day when guerrillas were most active.

The 2e BCCP was active in Annam until 12 December 1949 and on its return to France, Trinquier's pacification methods proved to be so successful that he was asked to visit two US counterinsurgency training centres in Korea and Japan.

Trinquier was sent to Indochina for the third time in December 1951 but on this occasion, it was as a member of the *Groupement de Commandos Mixtes Aéroportés* (GCMA), or Mixed Airborne Commando Group. Although this is straying into a narrative reserved for the second volume in this series on the First Indochina War, it is worth noting that the GCMA was a successor to joint British-French secret service operations in Indochina in 1944 (see chapter 1 of this volume). It is also worth mentioning that Trinquier went on to assemble an anti-communist, pro-French maquis comprising members of the Tho, Nung and Hmong peoples; another aspect of the war that was to have an influence on how the United States waged war in Vietnam.

The portrait of Roger Trinquier finishes at this point but a last anecdote makes him one of the most interesting figures in French military history. The back story to this anecdote

is told in the first of a two-part series dealing with the Congo Crisis,[10] when in January 1961, Katanga's Moise Tshombe asked Trinquier to take over command of his mercenary forces. This was at the behest of the French secret services acting for a French government that had designs on replacing Belgium as the former colonial power in central Africa in the early 1960s.

Aéroportées en Indochine (FAPI) led to the creation of two general staffs called the *Base Aéroportée Nord* (BAPN) and the *Base Aéroportée Sud* (BAPS). The creation of these units coincided with concerns that not enough attention was being given to the mobility of forces in and around Vietnam myriad of waterways, hence the introduction of the M29C Weasel in late 1947.

The Quest for Peace: the Bao Dai Solution

If the questions surrounding how much longer France could hold on to Indochina much longer pervaded French politics in 1947, the context in which these questions arose became far more complicated when in March that year, Malagasy nationalists launched a rebellion against French colonial rule in Madagascar. Although the insurrection cannot be compared in size and intensity to the one taking place in Southeast Asia, it did, on the other hand, mean that tens of thousands of French colonial troops had to be sent to the island over a two-year period and that a considerable amount of money would be spent attempting to retain the colony.

Colonial troubles such as this, increased the economic instability of France as it rebuilt after the Second World War. Added into the mix was a political instability whereby the French government was made up of a frequently changing coalition of different political groups including the French Communist Party (PCF). As witnessed through the actions of communist supporting French dockers who sabotaged aircraft and weapons shipments to Indochina, the PCF

The Emperor Bao Dai. Though his name meant the 'keeper of greatness', Bao Dai became known as the 'night club emperor' due to his spending much of the 1940s in this type of establishment in Hong Kong. (Author's collection)

strongly opposed the continuation of French presence in Indochina and demanded an end to colonialism in the country.

Opposition led to the PCF walking out of the French Assembly during debates on the future of France's future role in Indochina and more than once, blows were exchanged between supporters and opponents of the government's line. It meant that no definitive and immediate solution could be found to the Indochinese problem and the military stalemate would continue lest French forces receive the numbers of troops and amounts of material required to stand a chance of putting down the Indochinese insurrection.

The DRV understood France's position very well and continued to call for a peaceful settlement. In response and not wishing to lose face by simply withdrawing its forces from the colony, in April 1947 the French government drew up demands for peace that could not possibly be met by the Viet Minh, including the cessation of all hostile acts, terrorism and propaganda, the surrendering of weapons and the free circulation of French troops throughout areas controlled by Ho Chi Minh's forces.

The peace terms were rejected out of hand by the DRV, the French government concluded that further negotiations would be futile. Given that the French government did not have the sufficient political support necessary to send more troops to Indochina and to adequately arm these forces, it began to weigh up other options. The one that appeared the most feasible and the most promising, was to encourage the creation of Vietnamese political opposition to Ho Chi Minh and therefore, create political conditions more favourable to France.

The French quickly recognised that Emperor Bao Dai was perfectly suited to head such an opposition as he had the support of Vietnamese nationalist groups forced into exile in 1945 by the Viet Minh. These supporters including the Viet Nam Quo Dan Dang (VNQDD) and the future South Vietnamese leader, Ngo Dinh Diem who were also anti-French, as far as political purpose was concerned. However, the French (wrongly) expected him to be more flexible.

In the meantime, operations *Léa* and *Véga* sought to eliminate the Vit Minh from the equation. Although Operation *Léa* was successful in that it (temporarily) cut off the Viet Minh's supply lines from China, it cost an estimated 4 billion francs ($33 million) and the lives of over 600 French servicemen per month.[11]

As these figures were the cause of more consternation within French political circles and within France itself, the French government opened negotiations with Bao Dai on board a French cruiser anchored in Ha Long Bay on 8 December 1947. The French agreed to grant Vietnam independence with the French Union and it agreed that Vietnam should possess its own armed forces. However, the terms also stipulated that these forces should be made available to France if the need arose. Moreso, Vietnamese foreign relations would be managed by the French government and France would have preferential customs rights throughout the territory.

These terms were not acceptable to Bao Dai or his supporters as they did not grant full independence. Therefore, he returned to exile in Hong Kong to continue life as the 'night club emperor', a sobriquet he acquired due to his penchant for this type of establishment.

With negotiations reaching a new stalemate, French authorities made fresh attempts to engineer the appointment of a Vietnamese leader favourable to its ambitions by initiating talks with General Nguyen Van Xuan, the president of the provisional government of Cochinchina. These plans met Bao Dai's approval and that of the various nationalist groups but when Van Xuan put together a government to head the Provisional Central Government of Vietnam, they refused to lend it any support.

Nonetheless, Van Xuan's regime was confirmed as the ruling power of an independent Vietnam in Hanoi on 6 June 1948 and with this confirmation, France safeguarded the future of the French Union, a compromise that appeared to suit all the nationalist movements involved – apart from the Viet Minh.

Neither did the existence of Van Xuan's regime meet the approval of the French National Assembly; some of its more conservative members believed that an independent entity within the French Union would lead to problems in French North Africa, while others argued that 'independence' meant nothing of the sort, as the French Union still controlled Vietnam's armed forces and its economy.

The Van Xuan government gradually became seen as a puppet regime of the French. Their man in Saigon had not been given a mandate by the Vietnamese people or the governors of Vietnam's provinces in other regions of the country. Finally, after months of negotiations with the government of French President Vincent Auriol, Bao Dai agreed to sign the Elysée Accords of 9 March 1949. These agreements formed the basis for the creation of the State of Vietnam and stated that Vietnam would have greater independence within the French Union. By this, it meant that Vietnam could now conduct its own foreign affairs, control its own finances and possess an independent army. As for France, it was now seen as an appeaser in a national conflict that opposed the nationalists led by Bao Dai and communist factions led by Ho Chi Minh. As a result, the United States moved from a position of neutrality to one of support for Bao Dai.

1949: A Year that Changed the First Indochina War

Although the Elysée Accords brought renewed hope that Vietnam was veering much more towards full independence, the threat posed by the Viet Minh still had to be overcome. Nevertheless, political divergencies on mainland France meant there was still a good degree of unwillingness to commit more troops to Indochina. One solution was to lengthen the time troops spent in Indochina

Members of the Moroccan Tabor regiments. Though it is unclear if this photo was taken in Indochina, it shows the traditional garb worn by soldiers nicknamed 'goums'. Used as auxiliaries by the French, elite Moroccan soldiers such as this also served alongside the Spanish during their occupation of Morocco from the early nineteenth century. (Author's collection)

and naval forces saw their length of service in the conflict increase from 18 months to two years.

Such an increase was bound to have an effect on the soldiers' morale, health, discipline and operational skills so from early 1949, it was decided that the numbers be made up by increasing the number of indigenous and African troops, as well as an increase in the number of Foreign Legionnaires. This meant their numbers increased from nearly 12,000 in January 1949 to nearly 17,000 by the end of the year. The move enabled the reconstitution of the 5e *Régiment Etranger d'Infanterie* (5 REI) or 5th Foreign Infantry Regiment that served in Tonkin from November 1949.

As for colonial troops, the number of North Africans reached over 24,000 in December 1949, while the 'Senegalese' numbered just over 12,000.[12] The North Africans constituted 23 battalions (12 Moroccan, 10 Algerian, and one Tunisian), whereas there were nine battalions of Senegalese Riflemen. The Moroccan battalions included the elite Tabor, or *Goumier*, regiments that were to illustrate themselves in 1950 at the Battle for RC4. The name *Goumier* comes from the Arabic for unit, i.e., *Goum*.

As for the breakdown in percentages, 31.1 percent of the forces were European French (though many worked in administrative roles), 11.6 percent were Legionnaires, 16.7 percent were North Africans, 8.3 percent were Africans, and 32.3 percent were Indochinese.

Regarding which geographical areas of the conflict were given most attention, the priority was to stop the Viet Minh reoccupying zones cleared by the French throughout 1948. A task that was almost logistically impossible given that France never committed the number of troops necessary to cover the whole territory. Even if numbers had been sufficient, the Viet Minh had still not converted its effort to conventional means, so France's enemy remained largely invisible. Nevertheless, operations *Pomone*, *Jonquille*, *Pomone2*, *Canigou* and *Maurice* all took place in Cochinchina and Annam from early in the year and the French war effort was substantially strengthened in the north.

Due in part to the concerns that occupied the TFIS, in mid-to-late 1949 the contingents of the TFIN soon had to confront a completely new set of dynamics created by the triumph of forces representing Mao Tse-tung's Chinese Communist Party (CCP) over the KMT. Since January 1949, these forces had achieved a series of victories such as the Pingjin Campaign (29 November 1948–31 January 1949) and by mid-August 1949, the Chinese Civil War was just about over.

French observers were correct in their assumptions that a communist victory in China would greatly affect conflict in Indochina and stated that France should be prepared for a significant intensification of Viet Minh activity. They already knew that Tse-tung was supplying large amounts of military equipment to Ho Chi Minh's People's Army but now the fear was that China would serve as an enormous military rear base for the Viet Minh. Fears became reality when the Viet Minh began building larger arms depots to stock the increasing amounts of weapons supplied by the CCP and created transport companies that would ferry the weapons across the Chinese border with Vietnam. Moreover, in 1949, the CCP provided training to an estimated 10,000 Viet Minh regulars (bo doi).[13]

A good deal of time, money and energy was spent strengthening French positions in areas where it was suspected the Viet Minh would launch an offensive. These efforts were focused on reinforcing the north and northeast sectors around Lang Son and Mong Cai through movements such as Operation *Bastille* in July 1949. The objective to maintain control of the colonial routes 1, 2 and 3, in addition to not being able to fully counter Viet Minh ambitions in the area, the continuation of this type of security operation was beginning to weigh heavily on France's budget.

The cost of France's war amounting to some $500 million annually, fears were raised in the French Assembly that the war would not be able to continue for much longer. Certainly, France was in receipt of funds provided by the United States through the Marshall Plan but any money was needed for the reconstruction of France after the Second World War and not for the fighting of an unpopular war that was far from the priorities that affected the daily lives of most French.

What was to also change the dynamics of the First Indochina War was the albeit indirect, entry of the United States from a military point of view. Truman's administration was already concerned about the outbreak of a communist insurgency against British rule in the Malayan Emergency (1948–1960), now it confronted a situation whereby the whole of Southeast Asia was at risk of falling to communist forces. The fact that France would not be able to contribute militarily to the North Atlantic Treaty Organisation (NATO) was one thing, but it was quite another if it failed to contain communism in a strategically important area of the world. Soon, Truman and his successor Eisenhower, would have to react.

BIBLIOGRAPHY

Primary Sources

ALFSEA Operational Directive No. 12, 'Masterdom', 28 August 1945, WO203/2066.

'Directive by President Truman to the Supreme Commander for the Allied Powers in Japan (MacArthur), Instruments for the Surrender of Japan: General Order No. 1: Military and Naval', 740.00119 FEAC/4-1746

Giap, Vo Nguyen, *Military Art of People's War* (Monthly Review Press, 1970)

Gracey Papers, Gracey to Slim, Box 5/4, Liddell Hart Centre, 5 November 1945, in Daniel Marston, 'The 20th Indian Division in French Indo-China, 1945–46: Combined/joint Operations and the "fog of war" ', *NIDS International Forum on War History 2015*, National Institute for Defence Studies, Tokyo

Ho Chi Minh, 'To the Vietnamese People, the French people, and the Peoples of the Allied Nations', 21 December 1946, available at <http://www1.udel.edu/History-old/figal/Hist104/assets/pdf/readings/20hochiminh.pdf>

Ho Chi Minh, 'Appeal Made on the Occasion of the Founding of the Indochinese Communist Party', Hong Kong, 18 February 1930, available at: <https://www.marxists.org/reference/archive/ho-chi-minh/works/1930/02/18.htm>

Ho Chi Minh, 'Declaration of Independence, Democratic Republic of Vietnam', 2 September 1945, available at: <http://mprapush.weebly.com/uploads/2/9/3/0/29308547/vietnamesedocs.pdf>

Lieutenant-Colonel de Sairigné, Commandant la 13e DBLE, Secteur de Hoc Mon, 'Compte-rendu d'Opération Véga', 23 Februray 1948, SHAT, carton 10H4950

SEAC Joint Planning Staff entitled 'Force Plan 1: Occupation of French Indo-China' issued in 31 August 1945, WO203/5444

Service Historique de l'Armée de terre (SHAT), Box 10H984, General Georges Nyo, No. 73/3.S, 'Instruction sur la conduite de l'action politique et militaire dans la zone Cochinchine – Sud Annam', 14 March 1946

SHAT, box 10H 2283, note 708/FFEO, 22 June 1949

Telegram 851G.00/8-246, 'The Ambassador in France (Caffery) to the Secretary of State', Paris, 2 August 1946, FRUS, 1946, The Far East, Volume VIII, doc. 3801.

Telegram 851G.00/9-1746, 'The Ambassador in France (Caffery) to the Secretary of State', Paris, 16 September 1946, FRUS, 1946, The Far East, Volume VIII, doc. 4671.

Secondary Sources

Bergin, Bob, 'The OSS Role in Ho Chi Minh's Rise to Political Power', Studies in Intelligence, Vol. 62, No. 2, June 2018

Bodinier, Gilbert, Le Retour de la France en Indochine:texte et documents, 1945 – 1946 (SHAT, 1987)

Bodin, Michel, 'Les Laotiens dans la guerre d'Indochine, 1945–1954', Guerres mondiales et conflits contemporains, number 230, February 2008

Bodin, Michel, '1949 en Indochine, un tournant ?', Guerres modernes et conflits contemporains, No. 236, April 2009

Boissarie, Delphine, "Indochina during World War II: An Economy under Japanese Control, in Marcel Boldorf,and Tetsuji Okazaki (eds.), Economies Under Occupation: The Hegemony of Nazi Germany and Imperial Japan in World War II (London: Routeledge, 2015)

Bullit, William C. 'The Saddest War', Life Magazine, 29 December 1947

Cadeau, Ivan, La Guerre d'Indochine: de l'Indochine française aux adieux à Saigon, 1940–1956 (Paris: Tallandier, 2015)

Chen, King C., Vietnam and China, 1938–1954 (Princeton Legacy Library, 1969)

Conboy, Kenneth, The NVA and Viet Cong (London: Osprey, 2012)

Crosnier, Alain, L'Armée de l'Air en Indochine, 1945–1956 (Paris : Editions Heimdal, 2009)

Croizat, V.J., A Translation from the French Lessons of the War in Indochina, Volume 2 (Santa Monica: The Rand Corporation, 1967)

Currey, Cecile B., Victory at Any Cost, The Genius of Viet Nam's Gen. Vo Nguyen Giap (Potomac Books, 1997)

Dreifort, John E., "Japan's Advance into Indochina, 1940: The French Response", Journal of Southeast Asian Studies, Vol.13, No.2, 1982

Duiker, William, The Communist Road to Power in Vietnam (Boulder, Co: Westview Press, 1996)

Dunn, Peter, The First Vietnam War (C. Hurst & Co. Publishers, 1985)

Dunstan, Simon, French Armour in Vietnam, 1945-54 (London: Osprey, 2019)

Ehrengardt, Christian-Jacques and Shores, Christpher, L'Aviation Vichy au combat: Les campagnes oubliés (Paris: Lavauzelle, 1983)

Fall, Bernard B., Street Without Joy (London: Pen & Sword, 2005)

Garrett, Charles W., "In Search of Grandeur: France and Vietnam 1940–1946", The Review of Politics, Vol. 29, No. 3, July 1967

Goscha, Christopher E., Belated Asian Allies: The Technical and Military Contributions of Japanese Deserters, (1945–50)

Green, William and Fricker, John, The Air Forces of the World: Their History, Development and Present Strength (London: MacDonald, 1958)

Hammer, Ellen, The Struggle for Indochina (Stanford: Stanford University Press, 1954)

Marr, David G., Vietnam, 1945: The Quest for Power (Berkeley: California University Press, 1995)

McFall Waddell III, William, 'In the Year of the Tiger: the War for Cochinchina, 1945–1951', Ohio State University, 2014

Micklesen, Martin L., 'A Mission of Vengeance: Vichy French in Indochina in World War II', Air Power History, Vol. 55, No.3, (Fall 2008)

Rookes, Stephen, Ripe for Rebellion: Political and Miltary Insurgency in the Congo, 1946–1964 (Warwick: Helion & Co., 2020)

Shrader, Charles R., A War of Logistics: Parachutes and Porters in Indochina, 1945–1954 (Kentucky: University Press of Kentucky, 2015)

Soumille, Jean-Claude, 'Les avions japonais aux couleurs françaises', Avions, No.78, September 1999

'The Joint Chiefs of Staff and the First Indochina War, 1947–1954', Office of Joint History, Office of the Chairman of the Joint Chiefs of Staff (Washington DC, 2004)

Tanham, George, Communist Revolutionary Warfare: The Vietminh in Indochina (Praeger: 2006)

Tertrais, Hughes, Le Piastre et le fusil : le coût de la guerre d'Indochine, 1945–1954 (Vincennes : Institut de la gestion publique et du développement économique, 2002)

Truong, Chinh, 'Documents from the August Revolution, Resolution of the Tonkin Revolutionary Military Conference', Translations on North Vietnam, Joint Publications Research Service, Vol. 17, No. 940, 19 May 1971.

Windrow, Martin, The Last Valley (London: Cassell, 2005)

Young, Marylin B. and Buzzanco, Robert (eds.), A Companion to the Vietnam War (Blackwell Publishing Company, 2006)

Other Digital Sources

Berube, C.G., 'Ho Chi Minh and the OSS', available at < https://www.historynet.com/how-american-operatives-saved-the-man-who-started-the-vietnam-war/>

'Circulaire de Nguyen Binh concernant l'attitude à observer durant les pourparlers franco-vietnamiens à Dalat (19 avril 1946)', available at <https://www.cvce.eu/en/obj/circular_from_nguyen_binh_on_the_attitude_to_be_adopted_during_the_franco_vietnamese_talks_in_dalat_19_april_1946-en-5c5e754a-d7f9-4038-9943-52d0d47ddf10.html>

'Fantastic Victory in the Early Days of French Resistance, 27 February 2013', available at <www.boadongnai.com>

Feis, Dixie Bartholomew, 'The OSS in Vietnam, 1945: A War of Missed Opportunities', 15 July 2020, available at < https://www.nationalww2museum.org/war/articles/oss-vietnam-1945-dixee-bartholomew-feis>

Forsgren, Jan, "Japanese Aircraft in Royal Thai Air Force and Royal Thai Navy service during WWII", available at <https://j-aircraft.com/research/jan_forsgren/j-aircraft_royal_thai.htm>

'Franco-Thai War: The Indochina Micro Campaign, 1940–1941', (1 May 2020), available at <http://warfarehistorian.blogspot.com/2020/01/franco-thai-war-indochinas-micro.html>

Hanyok, Robert, "Guerillas in the Mist: COMINT and the Formation and Evolution of the Viet Minh, 1941–1945". Paper presented at the 1995 Cryptologic History Symposium, available at <https://www.nsa.gov/portals/75/documents/news-features/declassified-documents/cryptologic-quarterly/guerillas_in_mist.pdf>

Hong, Hoang and Pham Quang Minh, Pham Quang, *The Japanese 'New Vietnamese' in Vietnam's Anti-French War (1945–1954),* available at <https://core.ac.uk/download/pdf/144468621.pdf>

Liardet, Jean-Philippe, «L'Indochine française pendant la Seconde Guerre mondiale», available at <https://web.archive.org/web/20120205122644/http://www.net4war.com/e-revue/dossiers/2gm/indochine-sgm/indochine-sgm-01.htm>

'Notes on Prisoners in French Indo-China', 27 March 1945, available at <http://www.mansell.com/pow_resources/camplists/other/SAIGON_POW_Camp_RG24Bx6.pdf>

'The Gremlin Task Force, Part 2', 2 June 2013 (author unknown), available at <http://www.aviationofjapan.com/2013/06/the-gremlin-task-force-part-2.html>

'Vought V-93S & V-93SA Corsair: Aircraft of the Royal Thai Air Force', available at <http://www.wings-aviation.ch/11-RTAF/2-Aircraft/Vought-V-93/Corsair.htm>

NOTES

Chapter 1

1   Jean-Philippe Liardet, 'L'Indochine française pendant la Seconde Guerre mondiale', available at https://web.archive.org/web/20120205122644/http://www.net4war.com/e-revue/dossiers/2gm/indochine-sgm/indochine-sgm-01.htm, accessed 7 December 2022.

2   John E. Dreifort, 'Japan's Advance into Indochina, 1940 : The French Response', *Journal of Southeast Asian Studies*, Vol.13, No.2, 1982.

3   David G. Marr, *Vietnam, 1945: The Quest for Power* (Berkeley: California University Press, 1995), p.15.

4   Delphine Boissarie, 'Indochina during World War II: An Economy under Japanese Control, in Marcel Boldorf,and Tetsuji Okazaki (eds.), *Economies Under Occupation: The Hegemony of Nazi Germany and Imperial Japan in World War II* (London: Routeledge, 2015), pp.232–244.

5   Adapted from various sources.

6   Purchased from Japan on 10 October 1940. Jan Forsgren, 'Japanese Aircraft in Royal Thai Air Force and Royal Thai Navy service during WWII', available at https://j-aircraft.com/research/jan_forsgren/j-aircraft_royal_thai.htm, accessed 2 January 2023.

7   'Vought V-93S & V-93SA Corsair: Aircraft of the Royal Thai Air Force', available at http://www.wings-aviation.ch/11-RTAF/2-Aircraft/Vought-V-93/Corsair.htm, accessed 2 January 2023.

8   Adapted from 'Franco-Thai War: The Indochina Micro Campaign, 1940-1941', (1 May 2020), available at http://warfarehistorian.blogspot.com/2020/01/franco-thai-war-indochinas-micro.html, accessed 3 January 2023.

9   Martin L. Micklesen, 'A Mission of Vengeance: Vichy French in Indochina in World War II', *Air Power History*, Vol. 55, No.3, (Fall 2008), pp.30–45.

10 'The Joint Chiefs of Staff and the First Indochina War, 1947-1954', Office of Joint History, Office of the Chairman of the Joint Chiefs of Staff (Washington DC, 2004), p.7.

11 'Notes on Prisoners in French Indo-China', 27 March 1945, available at http://www.mansell.com/pow_resources/camplists/other/SAIGON_POW_Camp_RG24Bx6.pdf, accessed 26 January 2023.

Chapter 2

1   Ivan Cadeau, *La Guerre d'Indochine: de l'Indochine française aux adieux à Saigon, 1940-1956* (Paris: Tallandier, 2015), p.103.

2   Peter Dunn, *The First Vietnam War* (C. Hurst & Co. Publishers, 1985), p.140.

3   'Directive by President Truman to the Supreme Commander for the Allied Powers in Japan (MacArthur), Instruments for the Surrender of Japan: General Order No. 1: Military and Naval', 740.00119 FEAC/4-1746.

4   SEAC Joint Planning Staff entitled 'Force Plan 1: Occupation of French Indo-China' issued in 31 August 1945, WO203/5444.

5   Dunn, *The First Vietnam War*, p.141.

6   ALFSEA Operational Directive No. 12, 'Masterdom', 28 August 1945, WO203/2066.

7   Gracey Papers, ALFSEA Operational Directive, No. 8, 23 August 1945, as quoted in Dunn, p.142.

8   Dunn, *The First Vietnam War*, pp.236-237.

9   Cadeau, *La Guerre d'Indochine: de l'Indochine française aux adieux à Saigon, 1940–1956*, p.103.

10 Gracey Papers, Gracey to Slim, Box 5/4, Liddell Hart Centre, 5 November 1945, in Daniel Marston, 'The 20th Indian Division in French Indo-China, 1945–46: Combined/joint Operations and the 'fog of war' ', *NIDS International Forum on War History 2015*, National Institute for Defence Studies, Tokyo, pp.3–9.

Chapter 3

1   The term 'two-stepper' comes from how many steps a soldier could take before succumbing to the venom.

2   Bernard B. Fall, *Street Without Joy* (London: Pen & Sword, 2005), p.27.

3   'Circulaire de Nguyen Binh concernant l'attitude à observer durant les pourparlers franco-vietnamiens à Dalat (19 avril 1946)'. See, https://www.cvce.eu/en/obj/circular_from_nguyen_binh_on_the_attitude_to_be_adopted_during_the_franco_vietnamese_talks_in_dalat_19_april_1946-en-5c5e754a-d7f9-4038-9943-52d0d47ddf10.html, accessed 13 March 2023.

4   Telegram 851G.00/8-246, 'The Ambassador in France (Caffery) to the Secretary of State', Paris, 2 August 1946, FRUS, 1946, The Far East, Volume VIII, doc. 3801.

5   Telegram 851G.00/9-1746, 'The Ambassador in France (Caffery) to the Secretary of State', Paris, 16 September 1946, FRUS, 1946, The Far East, Volume VIII, doc. 4671.

6   Ellen Hammer, *The Struggle for Indochina* (Stanford: Stanford University Press, 1954), p.183.

7   Martin Windrow, *The Last Valley* (London: Cassell, 2005), p.90.

8   Cecil B. Currey, Victory at Any Cost, The Genius of Viet Nam's Gen. Vo Nguyen Giap (Potomac Books, 1997) p.134.

9   Ho Chi Minh, 'To the Vietnamese People, the French people, and the Peoples of the Allied Nations', 21 December 1946, available at http://www1.udel.edu/History-old/figal/Hist104/assets/pdf/readings/20hochiminh.pdf.

10 Giap, *Military Art of People's War* (Monthly Review Press, 1970), p.86, in Currey, p.135.

11 Ho Chi Minh, 'Appeal Made on the Occasion of the Founding of the Indochinese Communist Party', Hong Kong, 18 February 1930, available at < https://www.marxists.org/reference/archive/ho-chi-minh/works/1930/02/18.htm>, accessed 1 February 2023.

12 William Duiker, *The Communist Road to Power in Vietnam* (Boulder, Co: Westview Press, 1996), p.64.

13 Duiker, *The Communist Road to Power in Vietnam*, p.66.

14 Robert Hanyok, 'Guerillas in the Mist: COMINT and the Formation and Evolution of the Viet Minh, 1941–1945'. Paper presented at the 1995 Cryptologic History Symposium, available at https://www.nsa.gov/portals/75/documents/news-features/declassified-documents/cryptologic-quarterly/guerillas_in_mist.pdf, accessed 20 January 2023.

15 Hanyok, 'Guerillas in the Mist: COMINT and the Formation and Evolution of the Viet Minh, 1941–1945'.

16 Chinh Truong, 'Documents from the August Revolution, Resolution of the Tonkin Revolutionary Military Conference', Translations on North Vietnam, *Joint Publications Research Service*, Vol. 17, No. 940, 19 May 1971, pp.1–7.

17 Currey, *Victory at Any Cost: The Genius of Viet Nam's Gen. Vo Nguyen Giap*, p.88.

18 Currey, *Victory at Any Cost: The Genius of Viet Nam's Gen. Vo Nguyen Giap*, p.88.

19 Bob Bergin, 'The OSS Role in Ho Chi Minh's Rise to Political Power', Studies in Intelligence, Vol. 62, No. 2, June 2018, available at https://www.cia.gov/static/a0c34085dfe487b73cc90c8a92bb077d/oss-ho-chi-minh.pdf, accessed 1 February 2023.

20 Bergin, 'The OSS Role in Ho Chi Minh's Rise to Political Power'.

21 Dixie Bartholomew Feis, 'The OSS in Vietnam, 1945: A War of Missed Opportunities', 15 July 2020, available at < https://www.nationalww2museum.org/war/articles/oss-vietnam-1945-dixee-bartholomew-feis>, accessed 1 February 2023.

22 Bergin, 'The OSS Role in Ho Chi Minh's Rise to Political Power'.

23 Bergin, 'The OSS Role in Ho Chi Minh's Rise to Political Power'.

24 Currey, Victory at Any Cost: The Genius of Viet Nam's Gen. Vo Nguyen Giap, p.91.

25 C.G. Berube, 'Ho Chi Minh and the OSS', available at < https://www.historynet.com/how-american-operatives-saved-the-man-who-started-the-vietnam-war/>, accessed 1 February 2023.

26 Clarke W. Garrett, 'In Search of Grandeur: France and Vietnam 1940–1946', The Review of Politics, Vol. 29, No. 3, July 1967, pp.303–323.

27 Ho Chi Minh, 'Declaration of Independence, Democratic Republic of Vietnam', 2 September 1945, available at http://mprapush.weebly.com/uploads/2/9/3/0/29308547/vietnamesedocs.pdf, accessed 2 February 2023.

28 Charles R. Shrader, A War of Logistics: Parachutes and Porters in Indochina, 1945–1954 (Kentucky: University Press of Kentucky, 2015), p.68.

29 Kenneth Conboy, The NVA and Viet Cong (London: Osprey, 2012), p.5.

30 Currey, Victory at Any Cost, p.82.

31 Hoang Hong, and Pham Quang Minh, The Japanese 'New Vietnamese' in Vietnam's Anti-French War (1945–1954), available at https://core.ac.uk/download/pdf/144468621.pdf, accessed 29 March 2023.

32 Christopher E. Goscha, 'Belated Asian Allies: The Technical and Military Contributions of Japanese Deserters', (1945–50), in Marylin B. Young and Robert Buzzanco (eds.), A Companion to the Vietnam War (Blackwell Publishing Company, 2006).

33 Shrader, A War of Logistics: Parachutes and Porters in Indochina, 1945–1954, p.205.

34 King C. Chen, Vietnam and China, 1938–1954 (Princeton Legacy Library, 1969), p.262.

35 George Tanham, Communist Revolutionary Warfare: The Vietminh in Indochina (Praeger: 2006), p.68, in Shrader, p.206.

36 Service Historique de l'Armée de terre (SHAT), Box 10H984, General Georges Nyo, No. 73/3. S, 'Instruction sur la conduite de l'action politique et militaire dans la zone Cochinchine – Sud Annam', 14 March 1946, in William McFall Waddell III, 'In the Year of the Tiger: the War for <Cochinchina, 1945–1951', Ohio State University, 2014, p.133.

37 Gilbert Bodinier, Le Retour de la France en Indochine : texte et documents, 1945 – 1946 (SHAT, 1987), p.70.

38 Taoism is a belief based on Chinese traditions and religions. Taoists emphasise living in harmony with the Dao, the source, for them, of everything in the universe.

39 Cadeau, La Guerre d'Indochine: de l'Indochine française aux adieux à Saigon, 1940–1956, p.148

40 Simon Dunstan, French Armour in Vietnam, 1945–54 (London: Osprey, 2019), pp.15–16.

41 Fall, Street Without Joy, p.28.

42 Alain Crosnier, L'Armée de l'Air en Indochine, 1945–1956 (Paris : Editions Heimdal, 2009), p.81.

43 Fall, Street Without Joy, p.30.

Chapter 4

1 SHAT, box 10H 2283, note 708/FFEO, 22 June 1949, in Michel Bodin, 'Les Laotiens dans la guerre d'Indochine, 1945–1954', Guerres mondiales et conflits contemporains, number 230, February 2008, pp.5–21.

Chapter 5

1 All tables adapted from Christian-Jacques Ehrengardt and Christopher Shores, L'Aviation Vichy au combat: Les campagnes oubliés (Paris: Lavauzelle, 1983), pp.140–143.

2 Jean-Claude Soumille, 'Les avions japonais aux couleurs françaises', Avions, No.78, September 1999, p.5.

3 Crosnier, L'Armée de l'Air en Indochine, p.5.

4 'The Gremlin Task Force, Part 2', 2 June 2013 (author unknown), available at http://www.aviationofjapan.com/2013/06/the-gremlin-task-force-part-2.html, accessed 4 April 2023.

5 William Green and John Fricker, The Air Forces of the World: Their History, Development and Present Strength (London: MacDonald, 1958), p.103.

6 The EMEO/GMEO or GMTEO was made up from detachments of the Groupes de Transport I/15 and II/15. The GMTEO was disbanded in August 1946 when it became GT II/15.

7 Adapted from Soumille, 'Les avions japonais aux couleurs françaises', p.17.

8 Crosnier, L'Armée de l'Air en Indochine, pp.17–21.

9 Crosnier, L'Armée de l'Air en Indochine, p.25.

10 Crosnier, L'Armée de l'Air en Indochine, p.43.

11 Crosnier, L'Armée de l'Air en Indochine, p.80.

12 Crosnier, L'Armée de l'Air en Indochine, p.85.

13 Crosnier, L'Armée de l'Air en Indochine, 1945–1956, p.98.

14 Crosnier, L'Armée de l'Air en Indochine, p.126.

Chapter 6

1 V.J. Croizat, A Translation from the French Lessons of the War in Indochina, Volume 2 (Santa Monica: The Rand Corporation, 1967), pp.116–117.

2 Lt.-Colonel de Sairigné, Commandant la 13e DBLE, Secteur de Hoc Mon, 'Compte-rendu d'Opération Véga', 23 Februray 1948, SHAT, carton 10H4950, in Waddell, p.173.

3 Waddell, In the Year of the Tiger: The War for Cochinchina, 1945–1951, p.15.

4 Le Monde, July 1947, in Hughes Tertrais, Le Piastre et le fusil : le coût de la guerre d'Indochine, 1945–1954 (Vincennes : Institut de la gestion publique et du développement économique, 2002), p.66.

5 Cadeau, La Guerre d'Indochine: de l'Indochine française aux adieux à Saigon, 1940–1956, p.172.

6 ''Fantastic Victory in the Early Days of French Resistance', 27 February 2013, available at www.boadongnai.com, accessed 26 April 2023.

7 Cadeau, La Guerre d'Indochine: de l'Indochine française aux adieux à Saigon, 1940–1956, p.173.

8 Cadeau, La Guerre d'Indochine: de l'Indochine française aux adieux à Saigon, 1940–1956, p.173.

9 ''Fantastic Victory in the Early Days of French Resistance'.

10 Stephen Rookes, Ripe for Rebellion: Political and Military Insurgency in the Congo, 1946–1964 (Warwick: Helion & Co., 2020)

11 William C. Bullit, 'The Saddest War', Life Magazine, 29 December 1947, pp.64–66, in The Joint Chiefs of Staff and the First Indochina War', p.26.

12 Michel Bodin, '1949 en Indochine, un tournant ?', Guerres modernes et conflits contemporains, No. 236, April 2009, pp.135–154.

13 Bodin, 1949 en Indochine, un tournant ?, pp.135–154.

ABOUT THE AUTHOR

Dr Stephen Rookes used to work for the French Air Force as a researcher and lecturer at the *Centre de Recherche de l'Armée de l'Air et de l'Espace* (CREA) in Salon-de-Provence, France. Originally from Devon in the UK, but now a French national, Stephen Rookes is the author of five books published by Helion, and the author of peer-reviewed articles in English and in French